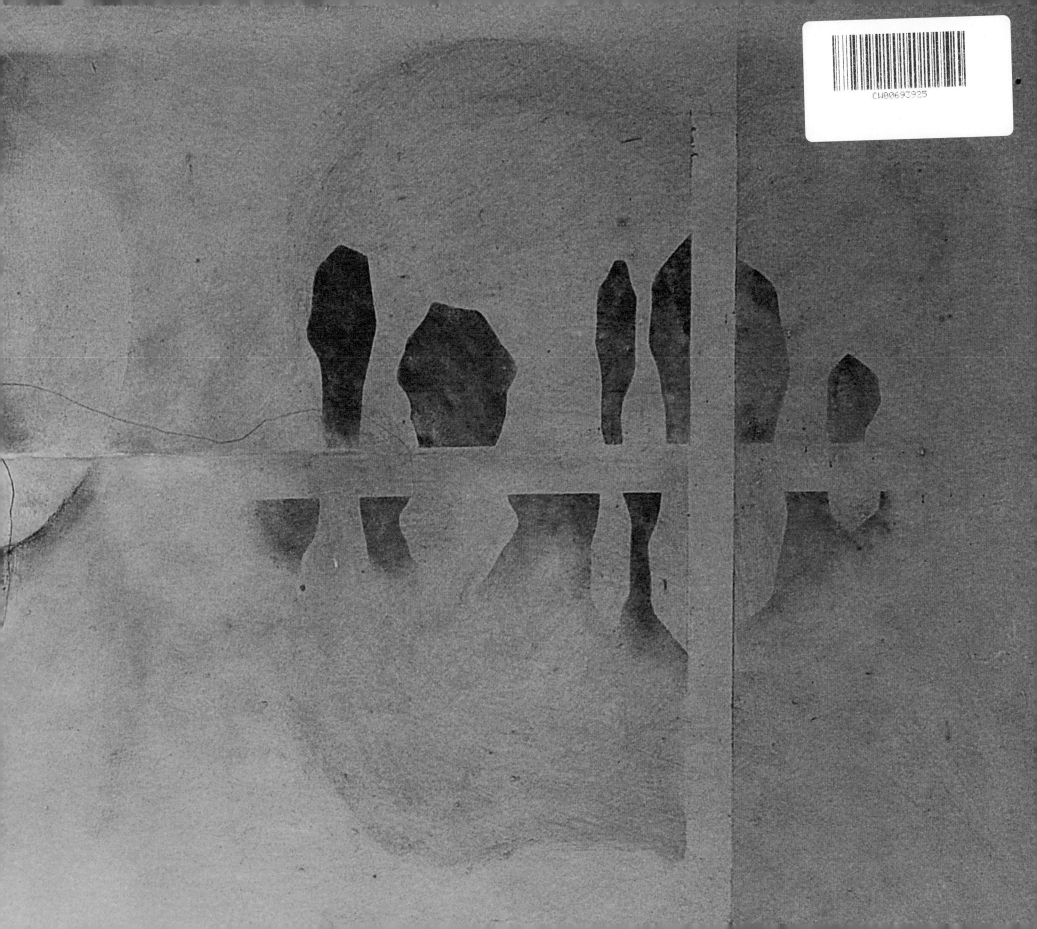

paul jones|overview

UNSETTLED EDGE · 51x50cms 2007

THE CANNON FOUNDATION

OVERVIEW · PAUL JONES
2010

Dedicated to the memory of James Robertson Bowie

With thanks to
VIVIENNE LIGHT FRSA
Fiona Robinson
Simon Barber, Evolver Books
www.evolver.org.uk

SARAH NICHOLLS · TECHNICAL SUPPORT

PETER SLADE · PHOTOGRAPHY
pcsphotographic@btinternet.com

Additional Photography
JAMES PHILIP HOWE & MICHAEL HALL.

Additional thanks to
Brian and Carol Graham, Michael and Janet Walker
Paul Light, Edgar and Janet Jones.

This publication has been supported by
THE CANNON FOUNDATION
The Cannon Foundation is a registered charity
committed to the support and encouragement of
arts related projects in the United Kingdom.

First published April 2010 by
CANTERTON BOOKS
Canterton House, Pitmans Lane
Morcombelake, Bridport, Dorset DT6 6EB
www.cantertonbooks.co.uk

Printed by
REMOUS LIMITED
Wyvern Buildings, North Street, Milborne Port
Sherborne, Dorset DT9 5EP
www.remous.com

British Library Cataloguing in Publication Data.
A catalogue record for this book is available from the British Library.

ISBN 978-0-9552266-2-5

CANTERTON
BOOKS

Paul Jones

paul jones|overview

The line drawn by an ancient hand
outlined that hand as well. Unique yet
universal, the hand then drew a line
that moved inexorably through time.

ART HISTORY

For Julie, Matthew, Sophie and Thomas

WITH SPECIAL THANKS TO
MICHAEL AND SALLY CANNON FOR
THEIR SUPPORT AND ENCOURAGEMENT

WITH THANKS ALSO TO
THE CANNON FOUNDATION

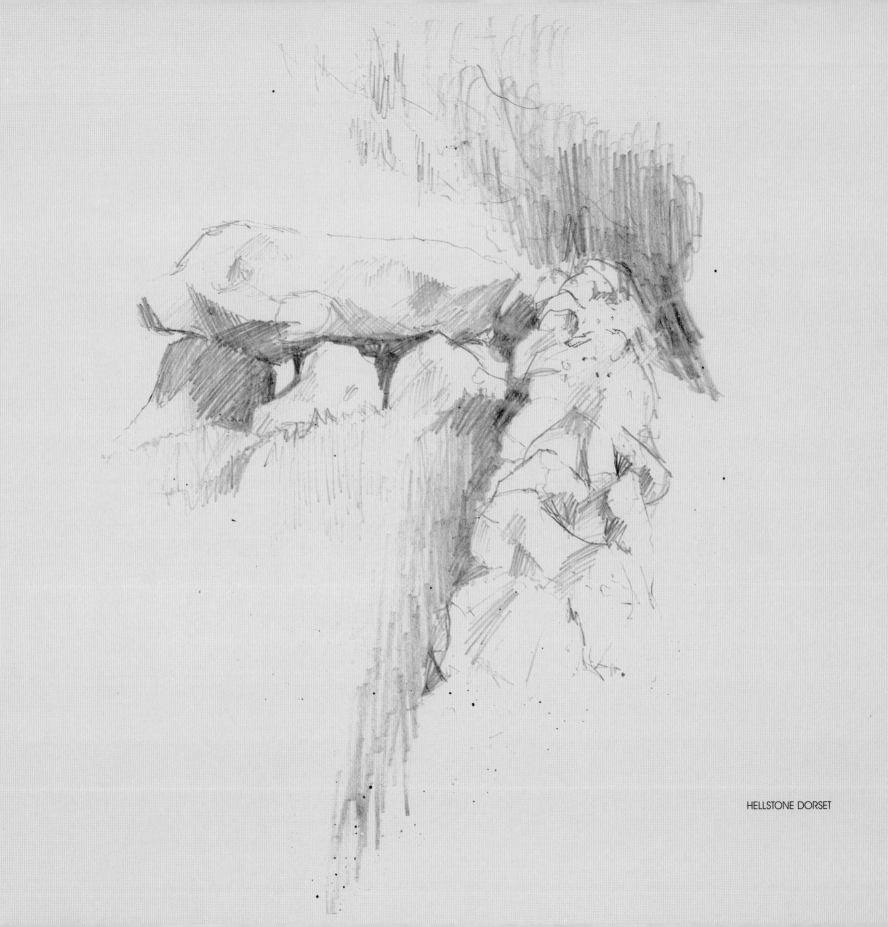

HELLSTONE DORSET

Overview

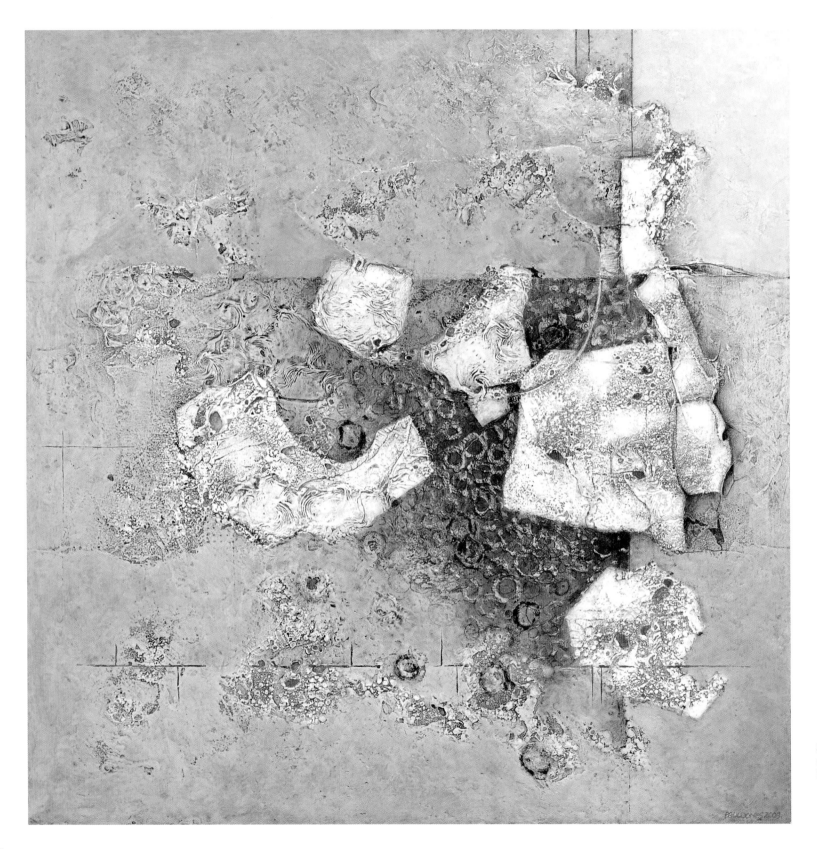

SEPARATION
60x60cms
2009

Contents

CRANBORNE CHASE 1999

HELLSTONE
DORSET
122x122cms
1977

Foreword

There is a stillness in the paintings of Paul Jones; his landscapes are lonely places filled with echoing silence. In the wake of Paul Nash he conveys the *genius loci*, the spirit of a place. His work is to do with the shadows which lie beneath the surface; the fragments and traces of human kind, of ancient history.

Particular sites are important to him. They are, as Roland Penrose once wrote, where 'one reality leads to another'. Jones uses the forms of landscape to invoke abstract notions of force, entrapment and entrancement. Beginning with the bare bones of land he explores its structural frame: its geology, history and human geography – its ancient habitats, chalk cliffs, field divisions, flint, tracks, stone enclosures even derelict airfields. These are places which continue to alter over time but resist final elimination.

From concrete beginnings, Jones' work evolves and takes on a life of its own. Rather than mirroring actual landscapes his paintings have to do with emotion and sensation – disturbance, discord, harmony, sadness. As a painter, Jones shows knowledge, strength, sensitivity and insight, and few can convey so powerful a sense of human connection with the past. He takes us to his own 'landscape within' and, placing us there, leaves us to solitary reflection.

Vivienne Light 2010

Vivienne Light has been active in art, music and education in both schools and universities. She is the author of seven books and in 2000 established the independent arts press, Canterton Books. An established artist and writer, she is a Fellow of the Royal Society of Arts and has curated exhibitions in the UK and Japan. She has also featured in arts based programmes on BBC Radio.

ENDFALL IV
51x46cms
2006

Introduction

Producing this book has been rather like creating a painting; I had a basic idea of what I wanted to achieve but felt that it should evolve naturally rather than follow a pre-determined course. Those of you who have seen my first book 'Signatures', will I hope forgive such repetitions as appear on these pages. This is a much more ambitious project and inevitably I want to include as much as I can. Simply, this book is an overview of the work of an artist who has spent much of his creative life painting, drawing and writing about the Wessex landscape. If you seek a category for my painting then semi-abstract would suffice, you will however discover both figurative and abstract images. We are never far from abstraction, isolate any section of the landscape and the abstract is created. It is that process of selection which is pivotal to this work.

The absolute basic requisites for any artist in my opinion are boundless curiosity and the ability to really see, not just to look but to perceive, evaluate, comprehend, record and create. This is an endlessly intriguing world and a constant source of inspiration. The more we explore and perceive the richer it becomes. If you are seeking the 'shock of the new', fashionable images of contemporary life, or political/religious comment, you will be disappointed. I have mentioned the principal resource for my work but you will find, as you turn the pages that many other themes have preoccupied me. Every painting is an adventure, unpredictable and challenging, exhilarating and frustrating. Nothing compares with that creative process, no piece is ever easy, nor should it be.

A variety of subjects have informed my work over the years but the core commitment has been to the landscape of the West Country and to the ancient sites and landscape of Dorset in particular.

DOWNFALL 2
33x33cms
2006

14

Introduction

Imagine a fine, dry day in late spring, a vast vaulted sky and a chalk textured field stretching ahead to reveal an ancient stone structure, a dolmen of nine vertical stones and capstone, the earth mound of its barrow almost completely eroded by centuries of exposure. The year was 1975 and this was the first of many visits to the Hellstone above the village of Portesham in Dorset.

I was not long in the county, having recently moved from the Midlands. I had been teaching there but with diminishing enthusiasm. At Corsham I had done well in graphic design and I decided that a change in career was due so I joined a Design Studio in Bournemouth. It was the beginning of a successful career and I eventually owned my own Graphic Design business. In the late sixties I had met Brian Graham, born and bred in Dorset and already an acknowledged and visionary painter. Always generous with his time and knowledge he was the ideal painter's guide to Dorset. That particular morning, discovering and drawing the Hellstone for the first time was memorable and very special. I still have those drawings, two of which are on pages 6 and 11. The site was the inspiration for a number of paintings (pages 10 and 28). The latter was inspired by a very hot, dry summer in the mid seventies when flames in the landscape were not unusual.

That period, the late sixties and the seventies, was a particularly exciting and creative time; being not only the foundation of a lifetime's work but a time for a special commitment as well. In 1972 I married Julie and that decade saw the arrivals of Matthew and Sophie, an exciting and creative time indeed!

It was 1979 when Brian and I shared our first major show at the new Arts Centre in Poole, now 'The Lighthouse'. The exhibition was timed to coincide with a Royal visit and being presented to Her Majesty was an unusual and memorable start to an exhibition…

NORTHCOTT
DETAIL
37x25cms
2008

Introduction

Having taught pottery as well as painting, the tactile quality of surfaces has been a strong influence on my work and texture is an integral component in each piece. In my paintings the actual application of paint is an exciting opportunity to experiment; layering, burning, smoothing, cutting into and marking, rubbing back, building up again and so on. The process continues until everything works. That's a special moment.

In response to the textures of the chalk/limestone cliffs of Dorset's coastline I experimented with various techniques. One of the solutions I had to keep in reserve until I had a separate studio away from the house. When you read the article on pages 141 and 143 by Fiona Robinson you will find that the experiment was reasonably successful, but that setting fire to paintings is a process best attempted well away from home! The process I use creates a contrast between textured surfaces and porcelain-like smoothness and at my exhibitions I encourage visitors to touch the paintings and feel the various textures.

I wrote in 'Signatures' that I enjoy listening to jazz and Miles Davis' work in particular. I have made a series of paintings attempting to express in visual images the rhythms, moods and 'colours' that characterise his music. Poetry has also been a strong influence and I delight in the richness of our language, there are so many poems that, to me, are paintings in words. My own writing is frequently in response to images and situations experienced when out walking or making drawings for a painting.

This is an 'overview' of the last forty years. Of the hundreds of pieces now in private collections, these are among the most representative. I hope you will share with me at least some of the pleasure that I feel in seeing these paintings, drawings and poems collected here together for the first time.

Humanity's shape,
carved by time in stone.
Sentinel standing and
guarding each other.

Back to back
around the circle of time.
Facing the future and
our curious examination.

STONES STANDING

Facing the Future

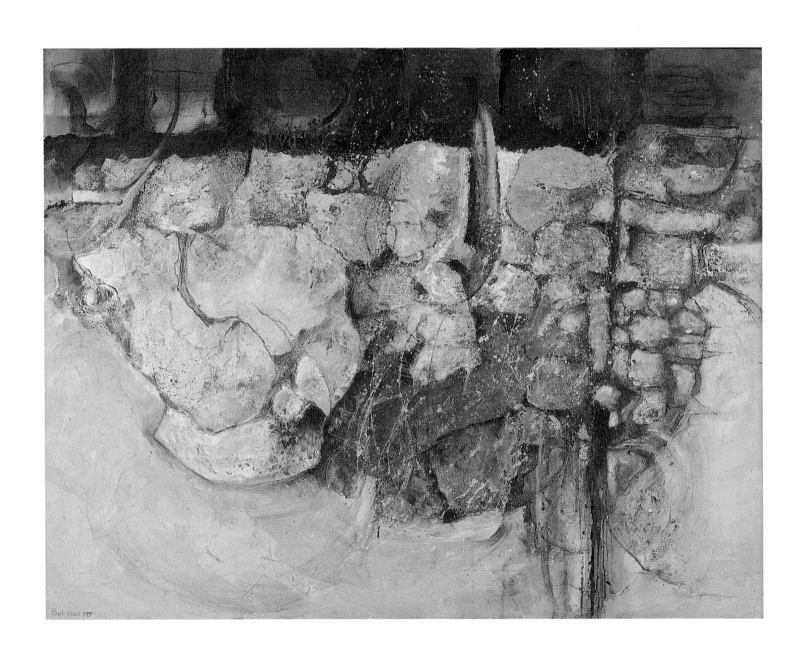

CHETTLE BARN 76x102cms 1997

Facing
the Future

In 1959 Rauschenberg was moving away from Abstract Expressionism towards the creation of his combine paintings and constructions. Jasper Johns was then developing his themes of flags, alphabets and targets. New York must have been an exciting, vibrant and innovative environment in the two post-war decades, with both art and music benefiting from the influx of creativity from war-torn Europe. This was the year a furious Lucio Fontana slashed his ruined painting with a knife and created a new genre of expression. In Rome, American painter Cy Twombly was producing his 'writings', a calligraphic form of marking the canvas like a wall of graffiti, and the Catalan painter Antoni Tapies was creating works that evoked elements that have withstood the ravages of time with his thick textures and smooth surfaces. In London we celebrated the work of Graham Sutherland, John Piper and Kenneth Armitage but we also became aware that we were on the threshold of a new era in art, music and design. Names like Patrick Heron, Francis Bacon, Peter Blake, John Bratby and Patrick Hamilton come to mind.

Why 1959? Because that was the year I left the stifling atmosphere of a country vicarage and arrived at Bath Academy of Art, which was staffed by Adrian Heath, Harry Mundy, James Tower, Gillian Ayres, Robyn Denny and Howard Hodgkin as well as many other eminent artists. Clifford Ellis, the Principal, had given me a scholarship which enabled me to study at Corsham, thereby creating a marvellous opportunity for me. Considering what was happening across the Atlantic and in Europe, the teaching was rather structured and insular but there were exceptions. Robyn Denny, a 'rebel' at the RCA was a keen observer of the American art scene, and an inspiring influence. He produced hard edged abstracts in beautiful colours, and impressed me with his huge typographical mural 'Great Big London' of 1959, an admiration which no doubt anticipated my later graphics career.

ELTERWATER
CUMBRIA
43x43cms
1990

Facing
the Future

It was a time of change. Change in art, music, film, fashion, literature and also in many areas of personal freedom. In retrospect it was like walking down a dark corridor into a floodlit room and almost anything seemed possible. It wasn't of course and it seems so defined looking back, but at the time it just happened, evolved. Exciting times…

One new freedom was that as students with money in our pockets we were able to travel more extensively and independently. We would go to Coventry to see the Sutherland Tapestry and John Piper's windows in the new Cathedral, to London's Cork Street and the Tate Gallery (when it was the only one in Britain) and to Manchester's Walker Gallery. Somebody was always going somewhere and if there wasn't any transport, we hitch-hiked. I had a good friend with a motorbike (for the enthusiasts, a Norton Dominator, later replaced by a Vincent Black Shadow) and we used to visit his home in Cumbria and from there, tour the Lake District. One unforgettable time we drove up to the Edinburgh Festival. He, like another good friend many years later, took great pleasure in introducing me to his beautiful county. We went there many times and I grew to love the Lakes. My affection for the area remains undiminished to this day. Tragically the motorbike that gave us so much pleasure was the eventual cause of his fatal accident when he was only twenty-four. My painting, top left on page 24, the poem and drawing on pages 30 and 31, were made in tribute to him. His photograph on the inside cover of this book, of me at Crummock Water was taken during one of our tours. In 1991 I had a solo exhibition in Cumbria at the Castlegate Gallery in Cockermouth and four of the pieces exhibited are on pages 22 and 24. I have returned to the Lake District a number of times with my family but nowadays the nearest I get to fell-walking is watching 'Wainwright's Walks' on television!

JRB AND
CASTLERIGG
CUMBRIA
122x122cms
1985

WASTWATER
CUMBRIA
122x122cms
1987

STOCKLEY
BRIDGE
BORROWDALE
CUMBRIA
50x50cms
1990

DERWENT WATER
CUMBRIA
50x50cms
1990

NR. POXWELL
DORSET
122x122cms
1989

NR. POXWELL 2
DORSET
50x50cms
1990

MANSWOOD
DORSET
50x50cms
1990

CRANBORNE
CHASE
50x50cms
1990

25

Paul Jones 1995

TARRANT VALLEY
DORSET
51x38cms
1995

Facing the Future

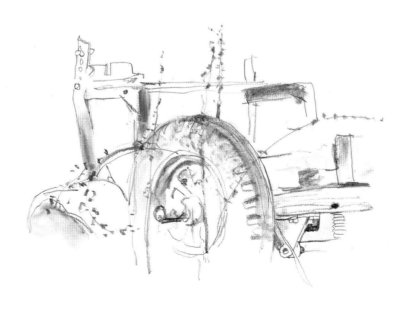

I discovered a real sense of peace in the Lake District. In those halcyon days it was possible to get away from the crowds and we would often walk all day, meeting only sheep and occasional walkers. When I moved to Dorset I found a similarly peaceful area near my home. Its quiet beauty and extraordinary history have been major sources of inspiration ever since I first visited it. I shall describe Cranborne Chase and its history later on but for the moment it is as a particular interest of mine and the subject for many paintings that I should like to examine it. Apart from a few small villages the area is basically chalk downland with a number of farms and some old abandoned barns and buildings. I am fascinated by the process whereby uninhibited nature takes possession of uninhabited buildings or anything else that man has built and neglected. Plants force their way through concrete and tiles, trees thrust up from old fireplaces, window panes crack and break letting the elements in and the ivy out as it gradually takes control... rooves fall, exposing the skeleton of construction which in turn collapses. Slates and tiles make subtle colours in dark corners.

I used to visit derelict farms, spending many peaceful hours with my son Matthew or daughter Sophie, drawing the frequently complex shapes of buildings and machinery nearing the end of their existence. Paintings I made at that time are at the top of page 25 and a drawing is on this page. It was a sad end for the farms but they were fascinating subjects to draw and paint. An old stone hut inspired another painting on the same page. That old hut, like so many I have drawn and painted, is long gone. Some, like the barn in the drawing on page 57, are now completely renovated. Occasionally such drawings have an historical value. Detailed drawings I made of the interior construction of a very dilapidated mediaeval barn near my home are now held in the archive of Wimborne museum.

HELLSTONE   AVEBURY   MARTIN DOWN

ALL PAINTINGS 122x122cms 1977-1979

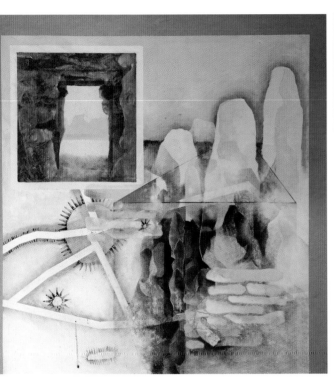

AVEBURY/WEST KENNET

HOD HILL

EARTHWORK

ALL PAINTINGS 122x122cms 1977-1979

An intimation of security arousing curiosity
A passing gratitude. A guide and tribute
Not tall, but strong and solitary
Braced against the wind and the toll of time.

Not just a careless construction
But twenty-four carefully crafted stones
No less – and no more.

THE CAIRN – FOR JRB

Facing the Future

Other times, drawings touch on historical events. During the war, Crichel Down on Cranborne Chase was requisitioned as a training area for the RAF. There are still the remains of a building from that time, a jagged, tile-covered shard of concrete floor jutting up at an angle, broken walls and intruding trees. I made a series of drawings and paintings based on the ruins. There was a famous case post-war when the owner of the Crichel Estate campaigned for the return of his land from the Government. Eventually he succeeded and in 1954 the Minister of Agriculture, Sir Thomas Dugdale took responsibility for his Department's actions and resigned. Not far from Crichel Down is the village of Wimborne St. Giles. Near to the village is an avenue of trees by Brockington Down where prior to D-Day in 1944, American troops were held in readiness, shielded from enemy aircraft by the canopy of elm and beech. While waiting and maybe to relieve the tension, they carved their initials and other images, including a pheasant into the tree trunks. I was still able in 1986 to make drawings of the surviving carvings, some of which are on pages 90 and 91.

When asked at that time to describe the work I was doing I would say that the paintings contained the most important images from a particular experience. Those images would then be reorganised to create a visual summary. For example, the central painting on page 28 was one that I made in response to a special day when I visited Silbury Hill, Avebury and the West Kennet Long Barrow. All three ancient sites were strong, graphic images which I placed against the background of fresh green which symbolised the Wiltshire countryside. I mention towards the end of this book how important these paintings still are to me as they are redolent with memories of an exciting period when art combined with archaeology and there was so much to discover and look forward to.

CAIRN 1990

WASTELAND
122x92cms
1994

Facing the Future

How fortunate we were to live in an area with such an ancient past and where the 'signatures' of man on the landscape, both ancient and modern, were, and still are a constant source of inspiration. This was a highly productive period and the foundation of a lifetime's dedication to the landscape, recording and developing the images of man's interaction with his environment. By man's 'signature' on the landscape I don't mean the influence of man in urbanising his environment but rather the physical marks he makes when working the land and adapting it to his own requirements, especially when it is a physical response to his aspirations and spirituality. This is a broad canvas which encompasses patterns simply created by working the fields, through to the constructions of spiritual or ritual significance. For example, the linear patterns made when planting or mowing and the magnificence of the megalith, dolmen and stone circle. It is the interaction between man and his landscape which creates the images which are a constant source of inspiration. The paintings on pages 28 and 29 are some examples of my response to this resource; others are on pages 58 and 70.

My home was a converted barn in a small village with a fountain in its centre. Hinton Martell is just off the road between Wimborne Minster (in 2009 recorded top of the Long-Life Table by the Office of National Statistics!) and Cranborne itself. The area within walking distance, about ten miles, determined the boundaries of my specific interest; an extraordinary area which includes both Badbury and Pentridge Hill Forts, Knowlton Rings, Ackling Dyke, the Dorset Cursus, Oakley Down and numerous tumuli and barrows. Archaeologically, Dorset ranks amongst the richest counties in the British Isles and to have so much and so near, was enough to keep an artist enthusiastically occupied for a life-time! I must have walked hundreds of miles during those years…

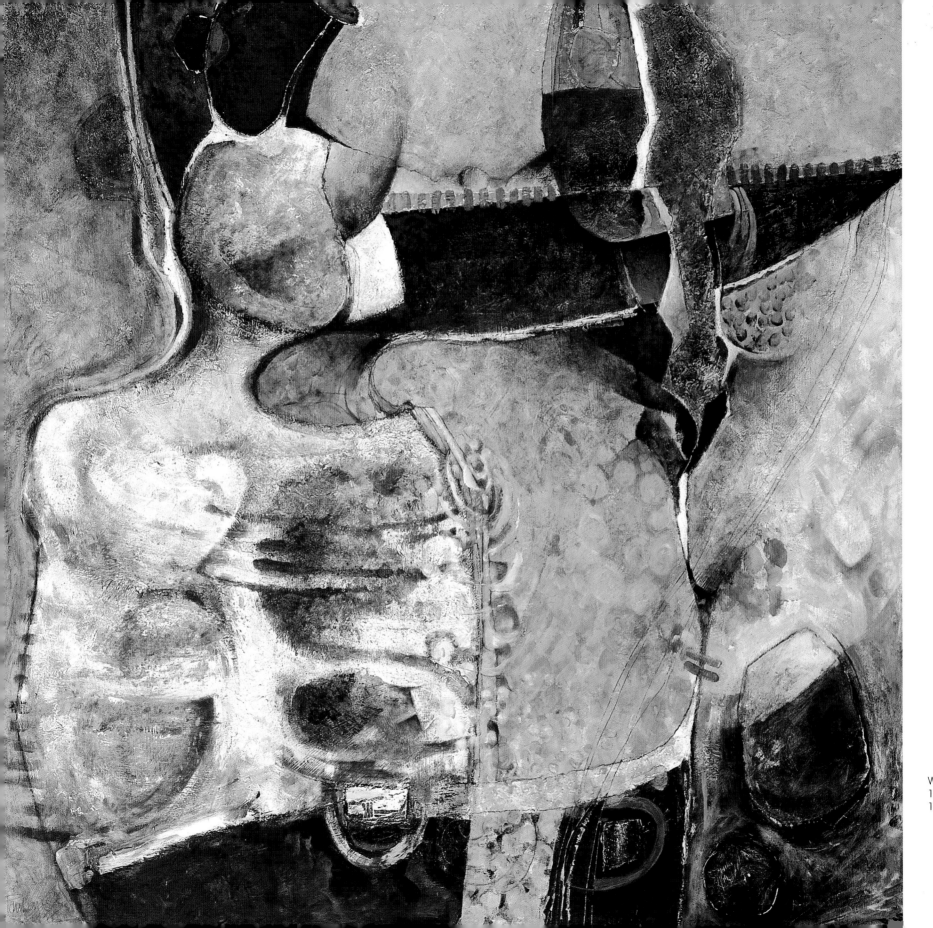

WASTELAND 2
122x122cms
1995

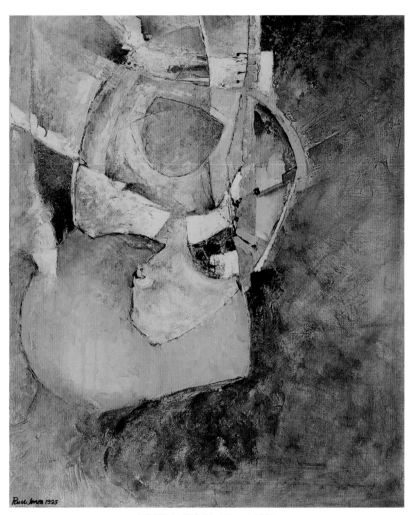

WASTELAND 3 76x64cms 1995

HEADLAND 51x40cms 1996

FIELD SYSTEM 2 25x35cms 1998

Facing the Future

I record some of my walks in my work book and supplement my drawings and notes with photographs. Although my work is no longer place specific, these notes constitute a valuable resource, as well as being reminders of many happy days. I enjoy the challenges of the area; a complex landscape, sudden ridges, downs, hills, woodlands and the chalk and flint soil that seems to reflect light from the huge skies. I have said how peaceful it is but it also has a very special atmosphere, a virtually unspoiled, ancient area, beautiful and rich in history. Almost everywhere are the signs of ancient habitation, all a gift to a painter on a purely visual level and one gets drawn into the detail; arrow heads and flint axes, burials and bones, knives and necklaces. The past is there for us to experience; the Neolithic through the Bronze and Iron Ages to those redoubtable Romans who captured Badbury hill fort and created Ackling Dyke, their direct road to Old Sarum. A rich and extensive resource is the research and collection of artefacts at Down Farm where Dr Martin Green has made a unique contribution to archaeology by making this area one of the most carefully studied in western Europe.

Referring to my work book, I note a typical day in March 1999, a cold, bright, early spring day. Julie drove me out to the Cranborne/Sixpenny Handley road and dropped me off where Ackling Dyke crosses en route to Old Sarum. I took time to enjoy the sight of Oakley Down, the spring sunshine accentuating the shapes of the barrows. Turning, I started my six mile walk home along Ackling Dyke, heading towards Gussage Down where I wanted to make more drawings of the barrows there for a new series of paintings. The day was sunny, spring gently asserting itself, and as usual I met nobody on the way. I used to meet a smartly dressed elderly gentleman in this area then, having missed his cheery greeting for a while, saw

A stone circle. Stones circling, something more, a truth,
A dance at the edge of the eye.
Too much to touch, so many shapes, deep shadows
Leaning into our hands.

Some time sun-time – grave and still we are.
Not them. They, hewn, weathered and worshipped,
Their backs to the sun, backs to the circling sun.
Back to front, sun to back to front.

A dance – a hesitation like a held breath.
Crafted, evolved, perfect and permanent.

STONES CIRCLING

STONES
CIRCLING
122x122cms
1978

WARMWELL TRIPTYCH 122x366cms 1980

Facing the Future

a memorial stone erected where the path crossed the Dyke not far from Down Farm. I often wonder if it was for him. I still give the stone a cheery greeting to this day; just in case, then I passed the gate where I once watched two hares leaping and boxing each other, a magical sight as they, oblivious of my existence, came to within a metre of me. Suddenly aware, they did a fair imitation of cartoon characters, leaping into the air and taking off, legs hardly touching the ground! Back on track, first left, past the Trig Point and head down the lane to the Barrow, the sparse hedges now showing off their new spring colours. I settle down to draw, enjoying the peace and atmosphere. Over towards the road I can hear the waspish whine of a remote controlled plane and it reminds me of when I watched a real plane, red and silver glinting in the sun against a vast blue sky as it 'wheeled and soared and swung'. I made a painting and poem about it (pages 42 and 43). My work done, I finished my afternoon by walking along the Dyke to Manswood and then on to Witchampton via White Farm and Sheephouse, arriving home as the evening began to draw into night'.

During the mid 1990s I re-read T S Eliot's 'The Waste Land' many times and I'm still trying to make sense of it. Recently I bought the recording read by Eliot himself and I agree that poets are not necessarily the best readers of their own work. I much prefer Ted Hughes reading Eliot. During the years since first reading the poem much had happened in my life and I hoped that advancing years would give me greater understanding. While it remained almost as enigmatic as ever, I did respond to these lines,

'Who is the third who walks always beside you,
When I count there are only you and I together...'

These two lines laid the foundation for a series of paintings including the four on pages 32 to 35.

A red and gold cross, glinting and spinning
in the vast vaulted sky beyond the veined trees;
before the sun, setting now for me, then for him,
sends the echoing cross into solitary silence.

SPINNING CROSS

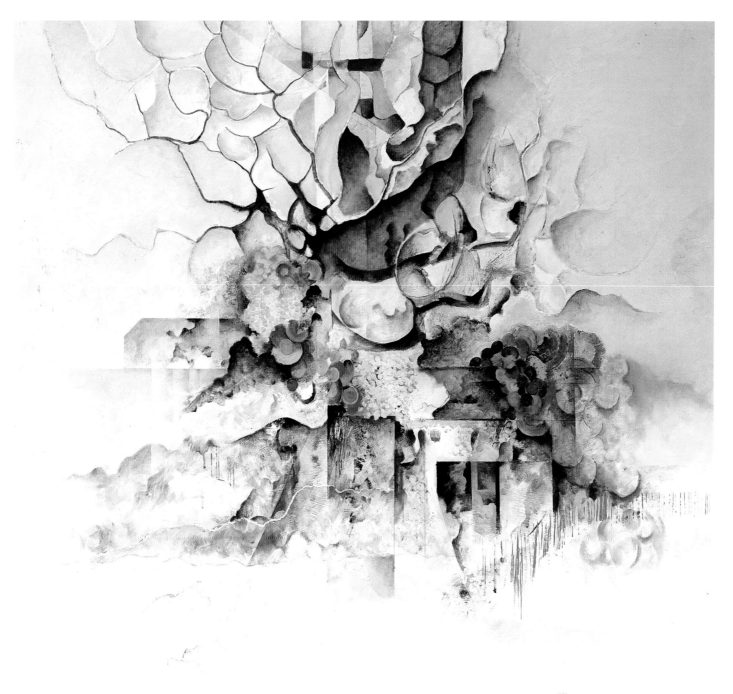

SPINNING
CROSS
122x122cms
1981

ROGER HALL DFC
122x122cms
1980

44

Facing
the Future

A programme on the BBC recently examined the concept of the 'other' person and gave examples of not only a passive companion but also one who was actually supportive in times of crisis. The scientists who contributed to the programme discussed research postulating that part of the brain is responsible for this 'illusion'. I am sure that the mind will sub-consciously interpret an abstract concept in order to identify it. An unusual shadow or juxtaposition of shapes can easily lead to misinterpretation, and many painters will have experienced the 'It looks just like…' comment about an abstract image they have created. However that is a long way from the 'other person' and being aware of another's presence, I am sure I am not alone in experiencing this phenomenon. The painting on page 32 responded to such an experience and it evolved sub-consciously. I had been walking all day by myself but had felt not alone. When the painting was developing I was aware of a central, almost Francis Bacon-like image and I developed this in Waste Land 2 on page 34 into two symbolic figures, then examined the concept throughout the series.

I rarely paint the human form. Occasionally, as above, I'll use a symbolic representation but in the series based on the Battle of Britain in World War 2 my respect and admiration for the people involved didn't allow for anything other than representation. I was born at the end of that fateful summer of 1940 and have always had an affinity with that period when, during a long hot summer, a small air force confronted a considerably more powerful enemy and refused to be beaten. That victory has been an inspiration ever since and one of my favourite paintings is Paul Nash's 'Battle of Britain', painted in 1941. Another is 'Totes Meer' (Dead Sea) of 1940-41. Nash not only produced some of the finest paintings of the First and Second World Wars but experimented with abstraction and surrealism. He had a profound love of the English landscape as well as

6ft6"x21ft OVERALL 1981

WARMWELL
DORSET
122x122cms
1981

48

Facing
the Future

being fascinated by flight. 1934 found him living in Dorset; his life and work during that period is well documented in Pennie Denton's book 'Seaside Surrealism, Paul Nash in Swanage'.

Dorset has a long association with aviation and I lived near Tarrant Rushton, famous as a wartime bomber base and most notably for its contribution to the D-Day invasion. However it was to Warmwell that my painter's eye turned and that old abandoned airfield with its decaying buildings became the inspiration for many paintings. At that time I read 'Clouds of Fear' by Roger Hall, one of Warmwell's Battle of Britain pilots, and we subsequently corresponded for many years. He visited our home and I gave him a painting of himself with his Spitfire (on page 44). An author and pilot I also knew at this time was Barry Sutton who wrote a powerful epic poem 'Summer of the Firebird' about his experiences leading up to his being shot down in the Battle of Britain. The poem was broadcast by the BBC in 1980 and was such an inspiration that I created a mural style painting based on it. Painted on seven door-sized panels it is (at 6ft 6in by 21ft) the largest painting I have ever done. It is on pages 46 and 47. My plan was to hinge each panel so that it formed a free standing semi-circle and have the poem relayed on a continual loop as a voice-over. I approached a number of venues but was told It would take up too much space… However, Barry Sutton was impressed and we had begun to work on an illustrated version of 'Firebird' when sadly he died. One of my drawings for that project is on this page.

All over the country lie old neglected airfields. Some almost completely absorbed into the countryside, others now industrial estates, a few still in use for private flying. There are a small number that remain almost untroubled by man and machine and are more or less intact. A visit now, when the mists shroud the earth, or

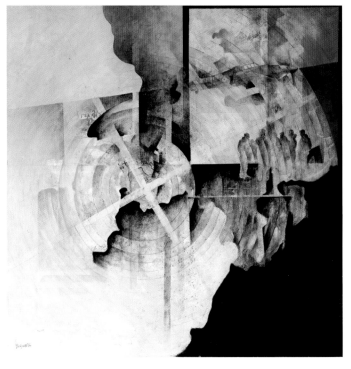

WARMWELL
DORSET
122x122cms
1980-81

Facing the Future

when the shadows lengthen into dusk, is full of mystery and memory. Warmwell, near Crossways in Dorset was then such a site, as was Rednal in Shropshire. I wrote a few lines about them as follows:

'Once busy with the sounds of machines and men, all is now silent except for the wind seeking out corners in windowless buildings. Derelict, roofless and empty these still bear the marks of their occupants, a broken sign, a Cross of Lorraine, a torn and faded poster. The rusted window frames surround the trees that with the years have grown through them and the mind searches the shadows in the crumbling corridors. Outside the mists shift on the flat field and one can imagine the almost tangible sounds of the past. Later, remembering, the memory is full of images, textures, metal, stone, space and the constant echoing hollowness of history'.

Eventually an even more ancient history began to exert its influence and human figures evolved into standing stones and dispersal bays into earthworks as in the 'Warmwell Triptych' on page 40. So the relationship of man with his land reasserts itself. 'Stones Circling' on page 39 is another instance of figure and stone symbolism which is complemented by the poem on the previous page.

In his 'Warmwell Triptych' Paul Jones has depicted it (the airfield) as it is now with nature taking it back on itself; as it was during the Battle of Britain; and standing stones providing a link with Neolithic times...the following quote from the Bishop of Salisbury seems apt, 'Tomorrow, today will be yesterday. History is but a moving line between the past, present and future'.

Iris Morris. Images of Dorset. Dorset Life 1987.

CRANBORNE
CHASE 2
40x26cms
1999

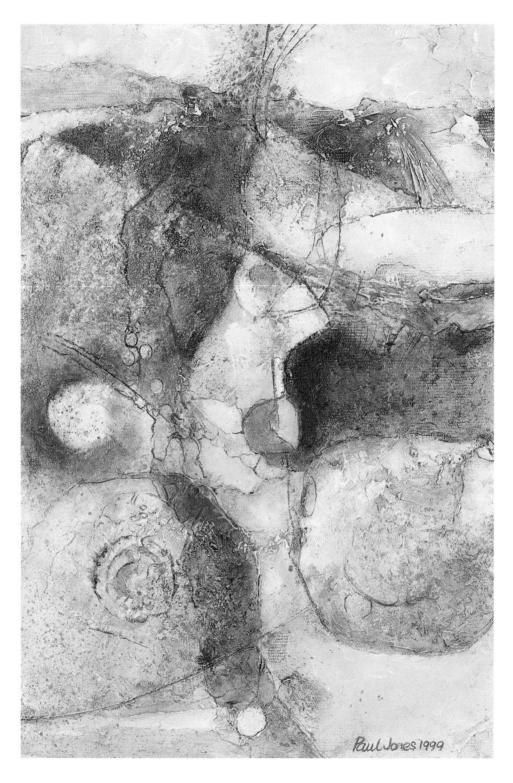

CRANBORNE
CHASE 3
40x26cms
1999

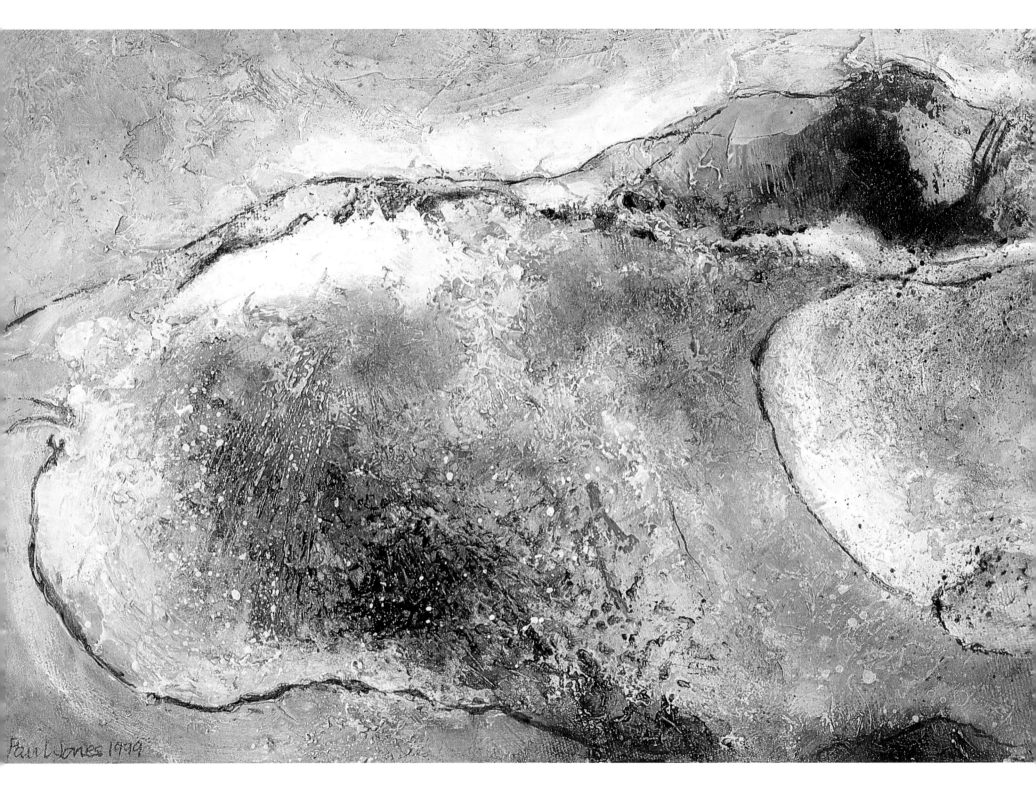

BULBARROW DORSET 25x30cms 1999

Facing the Future

The final paintings in this section bring us to 1999 and into a period more focused on landscape. I was soon to leave Dorset after thirty five years. Graphic design had become almost totally computerised and it was a good time to retire from the commercial world and be completely free to paint full-time. In 2000 we moved to a Devon farmhouse in a valley overlooked by nothing more than fields, trees and sheep, working in a barn converted into a studio/workshop and gallery space.

You knew that it was so – that when the probing wind
Shaped out the hidden colours in the space between,
It drew the spirit from the ground.
The clay beneath – a lifetime's work.
Now drawing on a distant past, the unseen hand
That drew the line was caught and pinned in layered time.

Beneath the dark an ever deeper darkness grew,
And so I thought when searching in the space between,
Below the shapes of time.
I saw the shadow of a stranger's face, a half-forgotten name,
An accidental meeting in another place.

The oldest and the simplest thoughts made new
By the very shape of things, heavy with the hint of truth.
You knew that it was so,
That when you pulled the image from the sky
Remade in hues of light and white and green,
The textures of the stones renewed, a loss restored,
You trapped and framed in space
The very essence of the place.

TIME AND PLACE

EXHIBITIONS 1978-1999

1978   West Row Gallery, Wimborne.
        One man exhibition.

1979   Poole Arts Centre, (Lighthouse).
        With Brian Graham, painter.

1988   English China Clays.
        Paintings selected for Conference
        Suite Project.

1989   J A Devenish.
        Four paintings commissioned for
        Brewers Quay, Weymouth.

1991   Castlegate Gallery, Cumbria.
        One man exhibition.

1992   Alpha Gallery, Swanage.
        Group exhibition.

1995   Upton House, Poole.
1996   'Best of Dorset' exhibitions.

1996   Wimborne Arts Festival
        Festival Artist. One man exhibition.

1997   Four Seasons Gallery, Wimborne.
        Group exhibition.

1997   Orchard Gallery, Bournemouth.
        One man exhibition.

1999   Four Seasons Gallery, Wimborne.
        With Peter Hayes, Ceramics.

BIBLIOGRAPHY ETC.

VISION. 50 years of British creativity.
Thames & Hudson.

The Crichel Down Affair 1954.

A LANDSCAPE REVEALED. Martin Green.
Tempus Publishing.

SEASIDE SURREALISM. Paul Nash in Swanage.
Pennie Denton. Peveril Press.

WINGS OVER DORSET. Leslie Dawson.
Dorset Publishing Company.

CLOUDS OF FEAR. Roger Hall.
Bailey Brothers & Swinfen.

PUBLICATIONS

1987   DORSET LIFE MAGAZINE
        Article by Iris Morris.

        BOURNEMOUTH EVENING ECHO
        Reviews of exhibitions by Jeremy Miles.

        DORSET MAGAZINE
        Reviews of exhibitions.

POEMS

Page 4   ART HISTORY
After reading about the hand paintings in the
Font de Gaume Caves, Dordogne, France,
I wanted to make a connection between the
outlining of those hands in 14,000BC; the similar
action undertaken through the ages, and the
development of that graphic line into
contemporary art. Simply, drawing a line
through history.

Page 18   STONES STANDING
Inspired by the stone circle at Castlerigg in
Cumbria this is a rather more introspective and
contemplative piece than 'Stones Circling' on
page 38.

Page 30   THE CAIRN
A tribute to my art student friend who lost his life
at 24. He had introduced me to the Lake District
and the enjoyment of Fell Walking, so the analogy
with a cairn has a special meaning for me.

Page 38   STONE CIRCLING
Also about Castlerigg Stone Circle. This wonderful
creation surrounded by majestic fells is an
awesome sight. Circling there, the stones leaning
towards the centre, or each other, it seemed to
me that they should be dancing.

Page 42   SPINNING CROSS
Written 'on site' in Cranborne Chase, this poem
was inspired by an RAF training plane looping and
spinning high above me, the wintry sun glinting on
its wings. Even when the dusk closed in on me the
plane was still reflecting the setting sun as it turned
and flew back to base.

Page 56   TIME AND PLACE
Written for Brian Graham about a painting I have
of his. It refers to shared beliefs, interests and deep
commitment to serious, contemplative painting.

GUSSAGE DOWN
DORSET
45x35cms
2000

Chalk and Flint

PARALLEL
INTERPRETATION
35x48cms
2000

60

Chalk and Flint

With the move to Devon, painting full-time became a reality. Gone were deadlines and the demands of clients; at last my days were my own to develop ideas. Fresh challenges and opportunities presented themselves on an almost daily basis. Most of all, there was time to develop concepts, to experiment and to work with new techniques and new materials. There was time also to explore that landscape within that had been gradually evolving over the previous three decades. To paraphrase: 'You can take the artist out of Dorset but you can't take Dorset out of the artist'. Thirty or more years had given me a 'library' of images that needed to be explored and expressed. I viewed the years ahead with great anticipation!

I've chosen the drawing on this page because in many ways it attempts to encapsulate so many of my interests. Pencil work obviously, then the subject I have already talked about, namely the transformation of man's creations/artefacts by nature into different entities. This piece of sculpture has been created by the elements out of a railway sleeper that once helped support a track of the Somerset & Dorset (S&D) railway network. It now stands as a fence post on the Bridleway above Down Farm on Cranborne Chase. Many others are to be found in the construction of barns and other agricultural buildings. Not so many have become beautiful sculptures like this one though. History is then included in this simple image. The S&D Railway was a casualty of the infamous Beeching Report of 1963 when nationally the railway network was cut by a quarter, 67,700 jobs were lost and 2,128 stations were closed. The S&D Railway finally closed in 1966, the tracks were removed and the sleepers' solid seasoned wood became a prime source material for farm buildings and fence supports. Time and climate have taken their toll on the exposed ones. Looking more and more 'Moore' like, this one's old bolt holes have opened up, creating

GUSSAGE HILL
DORSET
39x29cms
2000

WINDMILL HILL
DORSET
39x31cms
2000

FIELD SYSTEM 2
30x22cms
2000

Chalk and Flint

a wooden sculpture through which can be seen the landscape up to Melbury Down and Win Green Hill.

There are a number of similar hills in the area, dome-shaped and surmounted with a crown of trees. This gives them a certain character that has inspired a number of paintings. Possibly their attraction is because they are alike in shape to such hill forts as Badbury Rings. The 'Windmill Hill' paintings on pages 28c and 63 are just two examples of this interest. When we first moved into our house in Devon, it gave me great pleasure to see across the valley an almost identical tree-topped hill, Winscott Barton (pages 67 and 68).

Around this time I was exhibiting at Bettles Gallery in Hampshire, Maltby Gallery in Winchester, the Old Warehouse Gallery in Dorchester and at Bournemouth University's Atrium Gallery. Some of the galleries, notably Thomas Henry Fine Art, also took my work to London, to the 'Works on Paper' exhibition at the RCA and the AAF Fairs at Battersea. I enjoy exhibiting, the preparation, organising, curating (when possible) and being involved in the whole process. The best moment is being in the empty gallery and seeing all the work assembled together for the first time! I was being offered more solo shows, or rather, one painter, one potter shows. I have been fortunate to exhibit with many highly respected ceramicists such as Peter Hayes, Chris Carter, Ursula Morley Price, Peter Beard, John Bedding and Catriona McCloud.

The year 2000 was my first venture into producing my own book, 'Signatures', so called because it commented on my responses to man's influence on the landscape. My paintings at that time were mostly involved with landscape, as you can see in this section, but in due course an increasing proportion would be

GUSSAGE DOWN 2
DORSET
21x21cms
2000

WINSCOTT
DEVON
21x21cms
2000

FIELD WORK
35x45cms
2000

Chalk
and Flint

influenced by Dorset's 'edge', the extraordinary and beautiful coastline of Purbeck.

Cranborne Chase, like the countryside everywhere, is covered by a network of bridlepaths, pathways and tracks of all sizes, shapes and conditions. I call them 'Tracklines', a term that encompasses man's linear signature as he transverses or works the land, crossing the centuries as well as the landscape. How they all originated would make a fascinating study in itself. They include wide and varied examples, from the trivial to the awesome, the transitory to the ancient. Animal tracks, drovers' roads, processional ways, simple lines of vehicle and human access, bridlepaths, footpaths – the list is almost endless. At one end the Dorset Cursus and at the other, the wheeltracks of tractors. Generally most effectively seen from above, our undulating landscape offers many opportunities to appreciate the variety of patterns, stripes, loops, lines and circles that are everywhere to be seen on the land.

My earliest painting on the concept of tracks is on page 28 (Martin Down). The Martin and Tidpit Downs are just south of the A354 Blandford to Salisbury road. This is an area rich in ancient history, Bokerley Dyke is a great 'linear' fourth century earthwork that now forms the boundary of the Nature Reserve that is Martin Down. Pentridge Hill Fort and Tidpit Down are to the south, Windmill Hill (which I have previously mentioned) is to the east. This is wonderful walking country, (Map Ref. OS Landranger 184.SU01 18.50/4.90), with easy access from Cranborne or the A354.

Recalling that painting on page 28…one day I was standing high up on the Down and looking back towards a boundary gate I realised that the constant passage of cattle from all directions through the gateway had created an eccentric star-shaped pattern in the grass. That image I combined with

EARTHWORK 2
30x25cms
2001

Chalk
and Flint

Windmill Hill in the distance, contrasting the stability and structure of the hill with the movement and flow of the shapes and patterns created by the animals' actions.

You will notice on looking through this book that the subject of 'Tracklines' is a recurring theme; for example, the paintings on pages 73 and 84. More contemporary examples are on pages 151, 153, 158 and 166. Tracks and paths are an everyday part of our lives but to examine their function and physicality is a rewarding experience.

In my introduction to this particular subject I mentioned processional ways. On Cranborne Chase there is the Dorset Cursus. This is a unique construction of two parallel banks of Neolithic origin which has puzzled archaeologists ever since they became aware of it. Over six miles long, it was thought to be a race course or sports arena, hence its name. Nobody knows but it could have been a processional approach to the long barrows. It bears some resemblance to the great cursus at Stonehenge. Fairly close and actually crossing the cursus is the Roman road known as Ackling Dyke, which

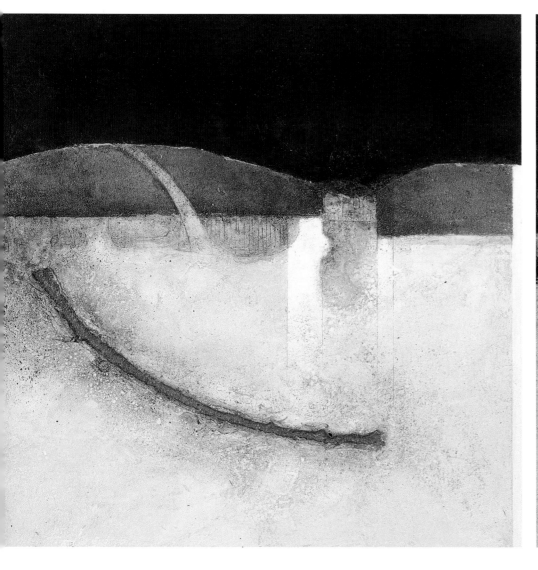

EARTHWORK STUDY 2
30x30cms
2001

LOOKING BACK 2
30x30cms
2001

FIELD SYSTEM 3
61x61cms
2001

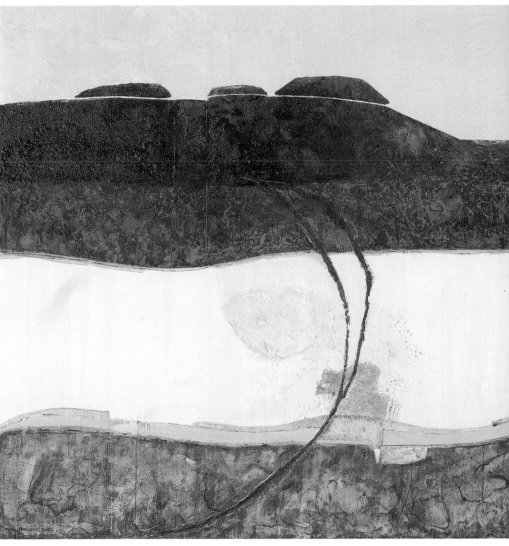

TRACKLINES 1
60x60cms
2001

GREENFIELD
51x51cms
2001

Chalk
and Flint

linked London and Exeter and was probably built in the period 55-60AD. From the Iron Age hill fort of Badbury Rings to Old Sarum, Ackling Dyke is acknowledged to be one of the finest stretches of exposed Roman road in the country.

Tracks which have inspired drawings, paintings and photographs lead to and from barns, farms and villages, their meanderings subject to the lie of the land, field boundaries and utilitarian needs. Each track has its own character and each one changes with the seasons. Closer examination will reveal the well-worn paths created by foxes, deer and other animals. The long barrows in this particular area also inspired a series of paintings, notably the barrows at Gussage Down which were the focal point of the walk which I recounted on page 37. These barrows are marked by animal tracks, as can be seen on pages 58, 62 and 66.

The archaeology and topography of Cranborne Chase are well documented and I have made suggestions for further reference at the end of this section. Many artists, past and present, such as Gwen and Augustus John, the Nicholsons and Stanley and Gilbert Spencer, have been associated with this area, all of them captivated and inspired by both its beauty and its history. As Brian Graham says in Vivienne Light's book, 'Re-inventing the Landscape,' 'The hinterland of Cranborne Chase resonates with the ancient past. The well-known, like Badbury Rings and Ackling Dyke make their own case, but just being in this unique landscape can be more than enough. Pre-history is all around, often beneath our very feet'.

I have titled this section 'Chalk and Flint' because it combines two important characteristics of this landscape. Some of my early years were spent in Herefordshire where the natural soil is, as here in parts of Devon, Red Sandstone. I find red to be the most

Arch of stone exposed
by the long incline of time.
Chalk and flint, bone.
Mound of earth long gone.
Tall grass, gaunt, rock heavy,
held by the clutch of sky.
Air, water, stone, then
scorched by summer fire.

REVEALED LINES (HELLSTONE)

Chalk and Flint

difficult colour to work with, though when I do use it as I have most recently with 'Hold the Light' on page 196, I enjoyed the challenge. The rich, red earth appears to me to be heavy and light-absorbing, unlike the Dorset soil which is predominately chalk, clay, sand and limestone. The chalk and flinted earth of Dorset seems to reflect the light and also produces fascinating tonal changes as it drains and dries, highlighting the fields from creamy-white to wet raw umber.

Flint invariably surprises with all the myriad shapes that form the natural stone. Many are the walks when I have been laden down with pockets and armfuls of flints! Sometimes they can be quite small but so attractive in their colouring and shape that they inspire paintings such as 'Flint' on page 154. That particular example was discovered by my friend Michael Walker when we were walking up to Tidpit Down. I have the stone on the desk in front of me now: one side of it has a uniform creamy-grey surface with no particular characteristics but the reverse is fractured and reveals a skull-like shape of graduated colour from dark brown and deep rich orange through to milky umber, surrounded by a pale grey border again surrounded by deep brown graduating to light brown with a touch of pink. All this in a small stone 55mm long! Another superb example is embedded in a wall of the ruined church on Knowlton Rings. Without a camera for once, I asked Michael's wife Janet to photograph it for me and I still find the colours in that flint quite extraordinary, so much so that I not only drew the stone (see page 200) but felt moved to write about it also, (page 184).

Yet another subject that deserves a book is the artist's studio. Every one is so different, ranging from total chaos to pristine tidiness and from garden shed to converted barn. Each one reflects the personality, work

QUAY
OBSERVATION
42x42cms
2001

78

LOOKING
BACK
61x61cms
2001

FIELD DIVISION
25x35cms
2001

Chalk and Flint

practice and individuality of the artist. For example, the studio of Francis Bacon, who knew where everything was in all the 'chaos' and Roger Cecil's studio, all completely monochrome, even the paint tins painted grey-green so there is no distraction from the work itself. Pristine tidiness is somewhat less common but I know artists whose studios are all white, with everything in its place and hopefully well organised. That's me then… I can't work in a mess but I do surround myself with 'finds' that I just have to keep. They are usually the unusual, things that are strange and intriguing, inspiring and beautiful. For example, there's a round white pebble that seems to glow, a badger's skull that appears to have come from an alien, the shell of a spider crab, a golf-ball sized 'paper' wasp's nest, beautiful in its fragility, a splintered and knotted piece of wood that resembles the beak and head of a raven, a stone that replicates the domed hills that I like so much and of course a collection of flints. It's also not just the article itself; each one has its history and its memories. For example, my daughter spotted the spider crab shell, a painter friend gave me a tropical seed that has eyes and a mouth like an alien creature, and I remember the walk when I first saw the stone that seems to emanate light. Other than in the 'Flint' paintings these objects are rarely found in my work but they are very much a part of my separate studio working environment.

Referring to the flint that Michael found, it's images like that stone that underline the basic principles of my practice: that is to say, 'My work responds to the natural abstraction that is all around us…I believe that if you isolate a segment of landscape, abstraction is inevitable and it is the selective process which is so valuable. Subtracting and abstracting from the apparently conventional creates a whole new world of images and continually inspires and challenges me to re-evaluate my responses.'

Fist of paper,
bud-like opens
in heat.

Flame caught,
thoughts burned.
Curling into black.

Letters make ash,
lost for ever.

So there's the
dream.
Suspended.
Flecks in light,
dancing.

FORGOTTEN LINES

SILENT
WORKING
45x35cms
2001

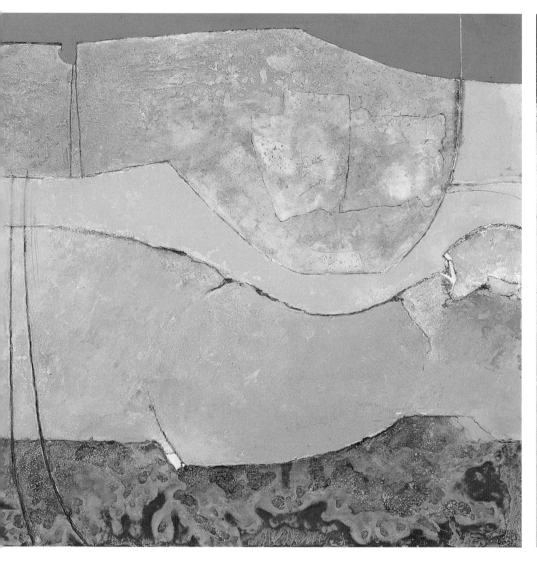

TRACKLINES 2
46x46cms
2001

BENEATH IT ALL
50x50cms
2002

Chalk and Flint

A painting will frequently develop in an unexpected direction. The decision then is whether or not to follow the original concept or to risk all and see what happens. Is the original concept so valid that at all costs it must be retained? One has also to bear in mind that the concept is based on previous experience and that to risk all is to move on…or fail completely. Personally I think it's always worth the risk, otherwise there's little progress. The advent of acrylic paint has transformed the whole process of painting and has made that element of risk less daunting. Not only has its rapidity of drying meant that a 'mistake' can be over-painted without delay but it can be rubbed down or scraped back to become a positive contribution to the work.

I never thought in my early years as a painter that acrylic paints would replace oils. The rich, glowing colours, the texture and smell of oil paint were so much a part of the pleasure of the painting process. How could this new 'polymer' paint compare with that? Actually in the early sixties acrylics couldn't, for example the surface, being slightly porous, was subject to atmosphere pollution and in time colours lost their brilliance. David Hockney's famous painting of 'Mr and Mrs Clark and Percy' (1970-71) is reputed to have lost some of its original vibrant colour. However, in time the advances made in quality have meant that acrylic paint is at least as brilliant as oil paint and is more flexible and faster drying. The latter property represents a hugely significant advance in the creative process, eliminating as it does the frustration of having to wait for paint to dry… All I need now is for some genius to make acrylics smell like oil paint!

RECOLLECTION – GREEN
20x30cms
2002

TOWARDS CRANBORNE
35x45cms
2002

That evening I remember was
so very still. Footfall the only sound.
Yours and mine.

Soft smell of night, cold and
quietly apprehensive. Clouds
leaning, heavy overhead.

Then the dark, thieving the bright
delight of Campion, Silverweed
and Thrift, leaving only the pungent
pleasure of damp perfumes.

Soft blues, yellows, greens and whites.
The lost last colours of the day.
Footfall the only sound.
Yours and mine.

NIGHT WALKING

CHALKFIELD
INTERPRETATION
61x51cms
2002

EXHIBITIONS 2000-2002

2000
Bettles Gallery, Ringwood, Hampshire.
With Ursula Morley Price, Ceramics.

Old Warehouse Gallery, Dorchester.
Group exhibition.

Atrium Gallery, Bournemouth University.
Group exhibition.

Maltby Art, Winchester, Hampshire.
Group exhibition.

2001
Four Seasons Gallery, Wimborne, Dorset.
With ceramics by John Bedding and
Catriona McCloud.

Old Warehouse Gallery, Dorchester.
Group exhibition.

Bettles Gallery, Ringwood, Hampshire.
With John Nuttgens, Ceramics.

Four Seasons Gallery, Wimborne, Dorset.
Group exhibition.

Thomas Henry Fine Art, London & USA.
AAF Battersea, London.

2002
Maltby Art, Winchester, Hampshire.
With ceramics by Catriona McCloud
and Andrew Davidson.

Thomas Henry Fine Art & Gordon Hepworth.
AAF Battersea, London.

Thomas Henry Fine Art, London & USA.
'Works on Paper', RCA London.

Old Warehouse Gallery, Dorchester.
With Silvio Vigliaturo, Glasswork.

Four Seasons Gallery, Wimborne, Dorset.
Group exhibition.

Old Warehouse Gallery, Dorchester.
Group exhibition.

BIBLIOGRAPHY

CRANBORNE CHASE
Desmond Hawkins.
The Dovecote Press.

DEVON'S GEOLOGY
Robert Hesketh.
Bossiney Books.

ROGER CECIL
Sarah Bradford.
Gordon Hepworth Fine Art.

A LANDSCAPE REVEALED
Martin Green.
Tempus Publishing Ltd.

EXPLORING ANCIENT DORSET
George Osborn.
Dorset Publishing Company.

RE-INVENTING THE LANDSCAPE
Vivienne Light.
Canterton Books.

VISION
50 years of British Creativity.
Thames & Hudson.

PUBLICATIONS

SIGNATURES
Book by Paul Jones.

Prior to embarking for France, American troops were held
in readiness under cover from enemy aircraft. While
waiting, some of the soldiers made carvings into the
bark of the protecting trees.

POEMS

Page 76 REVEALED LINES
On page 15 I have written about the
Hellstone. These lines describe, not only the
age and physicality of the stones, but also
refer to the long, very hot summer in the
mid seventies when 'flames in the
landscape were not unusual'. I used these lines
in the painting on page 134, simulating
carving in stone to make a point about
permanence in communication (page 137).

Page 82 FORGOTTEN LINES
The simple process of burning unwanted
papers and letters inspired this poem.
There is something poignant about the
process – words become ash and finally
just flecks dancing in the wind.

Page 88 NIGHT WALKING
One evening, in Yorkshire, Julie and I
walked along the narrow lane to the
village of Sedbusk. We saw no-one, the
dusk deepened into darkness and the air
became heavy with the threat of rain. The
silence of the night was almost tangible.

LATERAL MOVEMENT
28x50cms
2002

Drawing Inspiration

A solitary stone square
Beneath a cross.
Standing still and still standing
On the very edge of peace.

Gods, artists and tourists
And the occasional priest
Make light and colour
And muted conversation.
Paying their respects
Each in their own way.

ST ALDHELM'S CHAPEL. PURBECK

Drawing
Inspiration

On the Isle of Purbeck in Dorset and close to the edge of steep cliffs of Portland Stone stands an ancient chapel. Over one hundred metres above the sea, this solid, square structure has survived the worst of weathers since the 12th century, though the existence of an encircling earthwork hints at an earlier foundation. The chapel is dedicated to St. Aldhelm, first Bishop of Sherborne in Dorset, and was originally believed to be a chantry, where Mass would be celebrated for the safety of sailors. It was also reputed to be used as a haven for rest and prayer by such Royalty as King John, who not only hunted on Cranborne Chase but on Purbeck as well. The history of the chapel and its environment makes fascinating reading and I have suggested two resources for further reference at the end of this section. Over the years I have drawn and painted this small square chapel many times and have never ceased to be inspired by its position, history and atmosphere. It stands solidly on the southernmost point of Purbeck; beneath it are cliffs of Portland Stone and Kimmeridge Clay and above it the skies are huge, blending into the sea so that space and the elements combine to overwhelm and inspire the spirit. Services are still occasionally held in the chapel, the bowed heads of the tiny congregation dappled with the colours of the lancet window's stained glass. One such gathering gave me the idea for the poem on page 94 and on this page is a simple drawing of the chapel I made in 2004.

The 'Isle' of Purbeck is not of course a true island but a distinct region, the 'edge' of which is part of Dorset's famous coastline, a World Heritage Site. Rather than attempt to describe its complex geology I refer you to the official guide to the area, 'A Walk Through Time' edited by Professor Denys Brunsden. In the final section of this book I mention my preoccupation with the coastline of Purbeck, the extraordinary variety of its

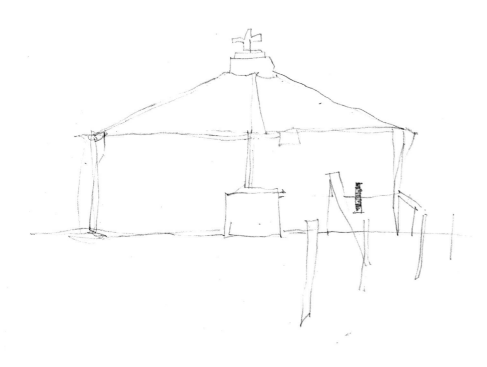

LOOKING
BACK 3
40x40cms
2003

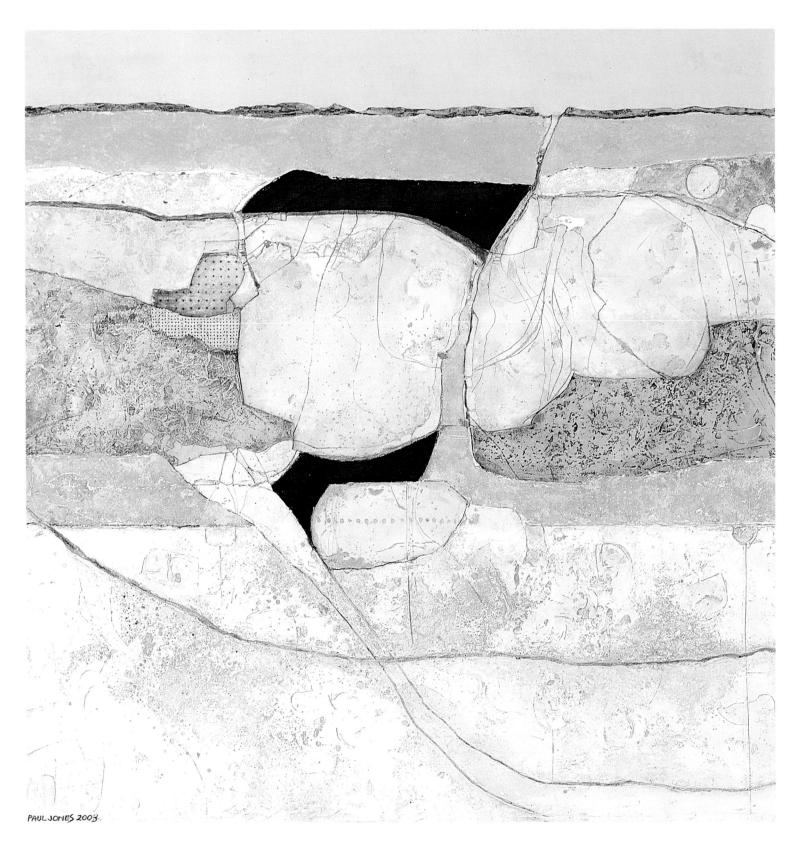

PAUL JONES 2003

LANDWORK
DIVISION
50x50cms
2003

CHALKSTACK 1
30x30cms
2003

LOOKING BACK 4
30x30cms
2003

CHALKSTACK 3
30x30cms
2003

Drawing Inspiration

geology, as old as 250 million years with the Mudstones and Pebble Beds of the Triassic through the Jurassic to the relatively 'modern' Chalk and Greensand of the Cretaceous period, a mere 65 million years old…. It is the qualities inherent in the chalk that give rise to my interest, its ability to reflect rather than absorb light, and its variety of surface textures. I remember one day holding a fallen fragment in my hand and realising that the minute fractured rock contained all the elements of the cliff that rose above me. My own coastline in miniature. When I taught pottery I was particularly interested in the various qualities of surface and how their varying textures could be achieved. Many years later, I am still preoccupied with expressing those values in my painting and feel that hopefully I am moving toward creating ceramic-like surfaces that directly relate to the chalk elevations of the coastline as well as the chalk and earth of the land. Regarding the 'cliff' paintings, it is the contrast between porcelain-like smoothness and the roughness of the fractured surface which forms a significant contribution to the work. There is of course much more to stimulate my senses; the cool, restrained colours, the contrast of mass and line and, as I've mentioned before, that specific quality of light which is complemented by the proximity of the sea. One other aspect of this and any coastline is the complex relationship of sea-edge with the elevation of the cliffs, the rocks fragmented, half submerged or briefly glimpsed as the waters rise and fall and also the changes of colour and tone and the lines defined by the movement of the sea. The painting on page 16, 'Northcott Detail' depicts this definition, the tide pushing foam, detritus and sand before it to create a defining edge. 'Northcott Detail', is actually a Cornwall based painting and is based on work I had done at Northcott Mouth, a bay near Bude. The rock formations and markings are quite extraordinary and well worth a visit with camera and work-book.

Chalkfall at cliff edge
A handclutch of history.
Rolled and tumbled by the sea
As if by potter's hand
In preparation for the wheel.

Spun and spinning and smooth
Each with its million shells
Minute and magnificent
Moving and irresistible.

CHALKFALL

Drawing Inspiration

The coastline of Purbeck with its switchback rise and fall was a major influence on my work during the 2002-2006 period and still stimulates and inspires. I have tried to rationalise the qualities that have informed my work and have formed the foundation of such pieces as those on pages 96 and 98. Here I attempted to resolve the relationship of lateral tranquillity in 'Looking Back 3' and the edgier elevations of the series on page 98.

Another aspect of coastal study is the relationship between sea and land. Does the land intrude into the sea or vice-versa.? With 'Looking Back 3' and the 'Coastal Observation' series on pages 102-103 the sea moves into the land, creating new shapes between the rocks, constantly taking and giving, eroding to build elsewhere. Very little stays the same for very long and one place's erosion can create some extraordinary responses. One summer's afternoon I was walking with friends along the shore between Swanage and Ballard Point. There at the edge of the water, and elsewhere caught up in detritus, were what appeared to be misshapen snowballs. They were in fact lumps of chalk that had broken away from the cliff. The constant ebb and rise of the tide on the shingle had gradually rounded the relatively soft material into chalk-balls…a sight so curious that I wrote 'Chalkfall' on page 100.

Virtually nothing stays the same. This is a restless planet, constantly evolving, constantly creating, surprising and intriguing. Small instances like the above, when the sea rhythmically moulds a lump of chalk into a ball, can fascinate and involve. The fact that the land's edge is continually eroding and depositing, informed a number of paintings during this period. Most of the pieces from page 104 through to page 111 are responses to this particular theme. With these paintings, not only was I involved with the movement, the downfall of rocks but contrasting that fall with vertical lines of construction.

COASTAL OBSERVATION
28x42cms
2003

COASTAL OBSERVATION 2
30x65cms
2003

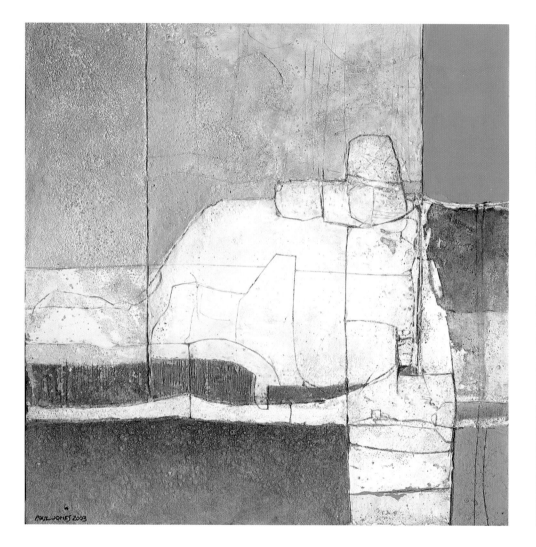

ROCKFALL 1
40x40cms
2003

HARTLAND ROCKS 2
40x40cms
2003

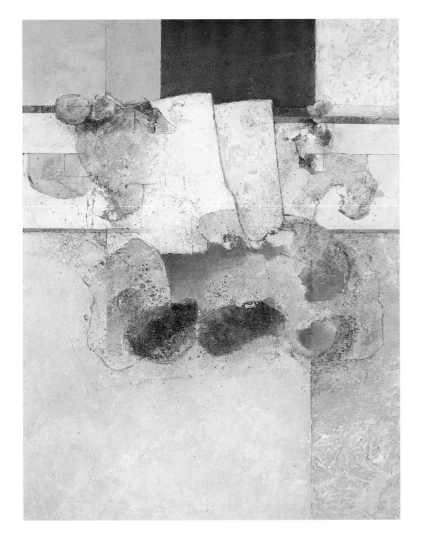

ENDFALL
50x40cms
2003

PARALLEL INTERPRETATION 2
50x40cms
2003

Sour smell of damp ashes
Acrid – somehow familiar
Somehow remembered
From an old experience
Almost forgotten.

Drawing inspiration
From that memory
That smell – I regard
The abandoned ashes
The forgotten fire
With wry regret.

DRAWING INSPIRATION

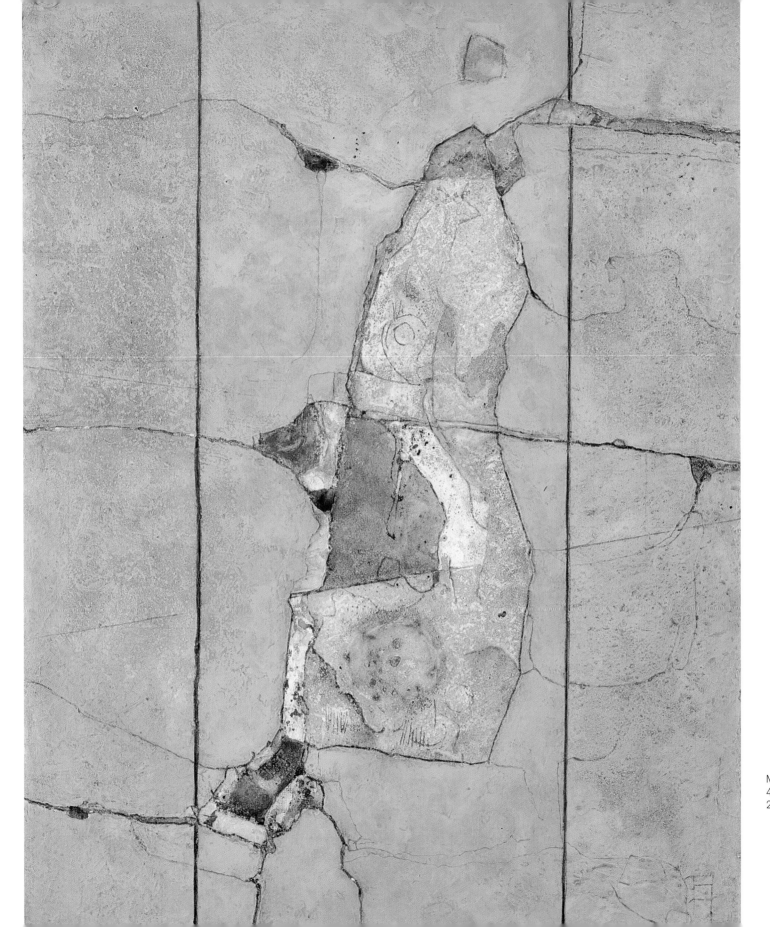

MICROROCK
45x30cms
2003

RECOLLECTION
50x50cms
2003

CHALK FORMATION
65x65cms
2003

CHALK FRACTURE
66x66cms
2004

ENDFALL 2
65x63cms
2004

ENDFALL 3
50x45cms
2004

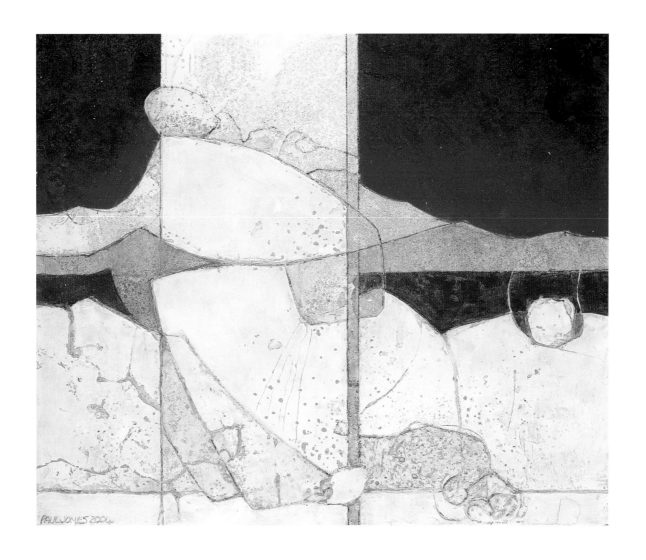

ROCKFALL (RED)
19x23cms
2004

FRACTURE
25x40cms
2004

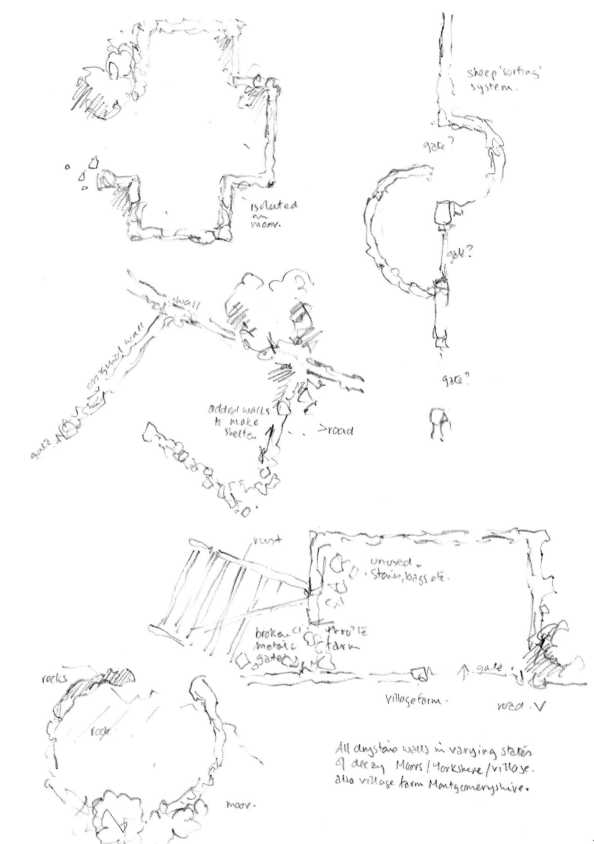

IMAGES FROM INFORMATION CARD ON SHEEPFOLDS ETC
FOR MY EXHIBITION AT MALTBY ART IN 2004

113

Clenched fist
tight on steel.
Subtle collisions
drive keen edge
into raw stone.
Making marks
familiar, abstract.
Shifting crafting
symbols, words
evolve & inform.

REVEALED LINES 2

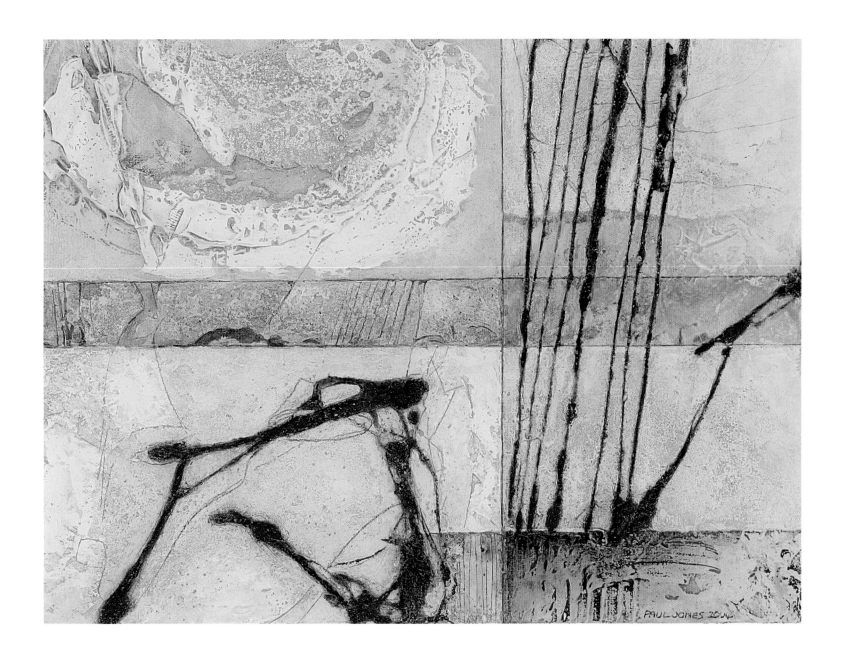

STONEWORKS
22.5x30.5cms
2004

SITE OVERVIEW
19x23cms
2004

AIRWORK
38x51cms
2005

AIRWORK 2
76x50cms
2005

AIRWORK 3
56x46cms
2005

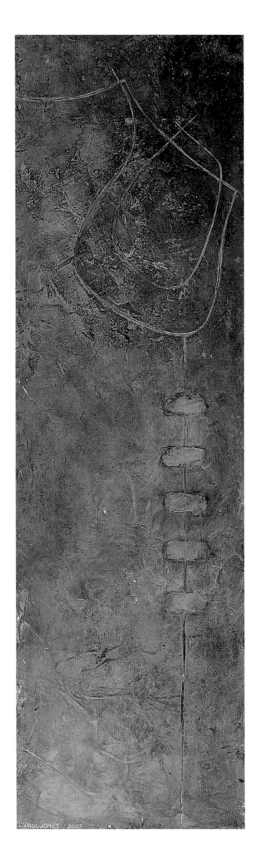

AIRWORKS
DETAIL 1
41x13cms
2005

AIRWORKS
DETAIL 2
41x13cms
2005

Drawing Inspiration

The winter of 2003 saw the first of many flights, by helicopter, from Devon to Yorkshire. It was those experiences that led me to explore a different subject altogether, the 'overview' of the landscape beneath that conditioned my perception from then on. I find the whole concept of flight fascinating, not only the miracle of physics that supports objects aloft, but also the sheer beauty and freedom of flight. The hawk hovering, a swallow slipping and sliding on the air, the graceful silent sweep of a white glider against the blue, and the overview of a landscape suddenly beneath, strange and ever new. It was that discovery that was so exciting…looking down onto a new world that was constantly changing.

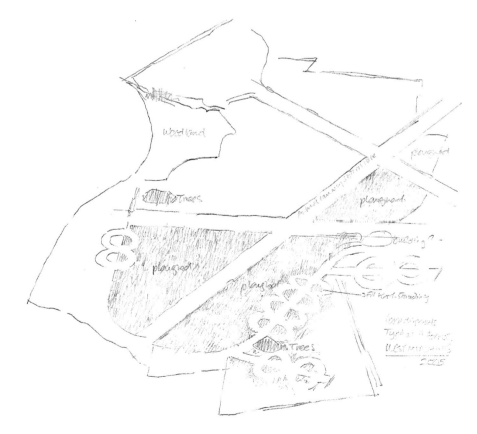

COASTAL
DIVISION
61x51cms
2005

Drawing Inspiration

My flights to Yorkshire gave me a new and exciting perspective on the land and coastline beneath. As a result, new images informed my work. The patterns and marks created by man through working the land; the effects of light and cloud on the landscape, endlessly defining and changing shapes with shadows and contrasts; the marks of ancient tracks and constructions, settlements and archaeological sites revealed in a dry season. The effect of man's impact on the land, both ancient and modern, is profound. It is also an unending and stimulating source of inspiration.

In 2004 I exhibited at Maltby Art in Winchester and chose 'Shelters', a theme inspired by the various designs of the sheepfolds I had seen when flying over the Yorkshire moors. The following are extracts from the exhibition's accompanying text.

'Flying by helicopter (an Augusta 109) between my home in Devon and Yorkshire was a revelation. Its relatively modest airspeed allowed the luxury of a close examination of the landscape, (the Augusta has a transparent floor in the cockpit so it was literally 'the land beneath my feet'). This overview revealed the commonplace as frequently intriguing and often beautiful. The landscape surrendered many secrets. Ancient sites, invisible from the ground, became evident…the endless complexities of the land kept the camera and work-book busy. This collection of work was borne out of the mundane, a utilitarian endeavour to protect livestock, the construction of a sanctuary in stone. The deployment of natural resources created the shelters and their design was often informed by their environment. Why a sheepfold should be built as a cruciform structure I don't know but it looked impressive on an exposed moor…. I explored other images of sheepfolds, creating a number of drawings which inspired most of these paintings'.

Falling water,
Foam white on
Scattered stones.
All corners and
Stacked sharp
Like broken pavers
Shiny wet and
Green as grass.

DOWNFALL

CHALK ELEVATION 3
61x92cms
2005

CHALK DIVISION 3
50x50cms
2005

Drawing Inspiration

The drawings referred to are on page 113, and I was reliably informed at the exhibition that the 'cruciform structure' is extremely strong. A dry-stone corner is very robust and multiplied by twelve will give safe shelter against the worst of weathers. The paintings I have selected from that exhibition are on pages 112 and 115. 'Stoneworks' on page 115 was also shown at the Bournemouth University's Art Loan Exhibition in 2004/5.

Sheepfolds were not the only discovery arising from those flights to and from the north of England. Two of my interests neatly came together when my fascination with airfields and archaeology unexpectedly combined. On an early flight I realised that certain straight tracks and field boundaries were not parts of Roman roads or similar, but when related to other straight lines indicated the landing strips of old airfields from the Second World War. Further examination revealed elliptical shapes either side of some of the tracks which were dispersal loops for aircraft on stand-by. Once realised, it is surprising how many old airfields have been absorbed into the landscape, only straight lines and symbols in the dry earth revealing their history. The drawing on page 121 was made from photographs I took in 2005, the extended A of the runways and the dispersal loops are plainly visible and formed the basis for a series of paintings, some of which are from page 116 through to page 120.

I enjoyed the challenge of making these pieces work, they were different from anything else I had done and required a completely different approach from which I learned a great deal. Their influence on my subsequent work is most apparent in 'Coastal Division' on page 122 which was exhibited in a new series of paintings of the Dorset coastline at Maltby Art in 2006.

LOOKING BACK – WINSPIT
38x38cms
2005

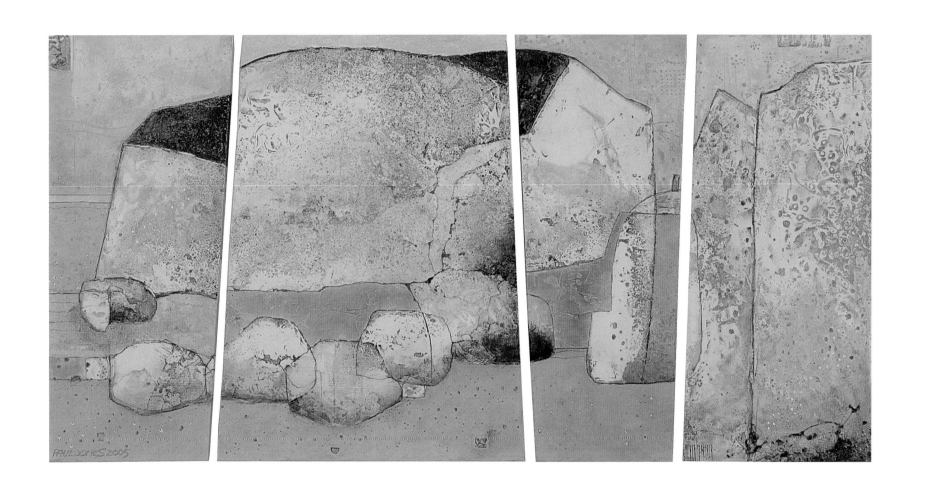

COASTAL SEPARATION
26x50cms
2005

CHALK
ELEVATION.RED
28x22cms
2005

CHALKFALL
92x61cms
2006

EXHIBITIONS 2003-2006

2003
Bettles Gallery, Ringwood, Hampshire.
With Peter Beard, Ceramics.

Thomas Henry Fine Art, London & USA.
AAF Battersea, London.

Old Warehouse Gallery, Dorchester.
One man exhibition.

Maltby Art, Winchester, Hampshire.
With Tim Smith, Sculpture.

2004
Sherborne House, Sherborne, Dorset.
Group exhibition.

Bettles Gallery, Ringwood, Hampshire.
With Brian Graham & John Leach.

Burton Municipal Gallery, Bideford, Devon.
One man exhibition.

Acanthus Gallery, Wareham, Dorset.
Group exhibition.

Edgarmodern Gallery, Bath.
AAF Battersea, London.

Bettles Gallery, Ringwood, Hampshire.
Group exhibition.

Edgarmodern Gallery, Bath.
Group exhibition.

2005
Edgarmodern Gallery, Bath.
London Art Fair, Islington, London.

Bettles Gallery, Ringwood, Hampshire.
Group exhibition.

Six Chapel Row Gallery, Bath.
Group exhibition.

2006
Maltby Art, Winchester, Hampshire.
With Chris Carter, Ceramics.

Acanthus Gallery, Wareham, Dorset.
Group exhibition.

Brewhouse Arts Centre, Taunton, Somerset.
Group exhibition.

BIBLIOGRAPHY

PURBECK. Paul Hyland.
Dovecot Press, Wimborne, Dorset.

CHAPEL OF ST ALDHELM. Wallace & Watton.

A WALK THROUGH TIME.
Edited by Professor Denys Brunsden.
Coastal Publishing, Wareham, Dorset.

BRITAIN'S MILITARY AIRFIELDS. David J Smith.
Thorsons Publishing Group, Wellingborough.

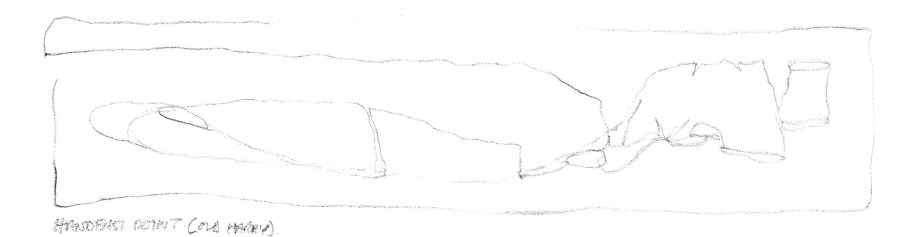

STRADFAST POINT (OLD HARRY).

POEMS

Page 94 ST ALDHELM'S CHAPEL
I have described the chapel on page 95.
The poem is about antiquity, tranquillity and
spirituality. Being on the edge of the land,
with nothing but the sea and sky beyond, is
somehow symbolic and I like the fact that
services are still occasionally held in this
simple and sacred stone structure.

Page 100 CHALKFALL
A retelling of the discovery, (on page 101),
of misshapen balls of chalk on the beach
near Swanage. Lumps of chalk had fallen
from the cliffs and being made of porous
limestone,(containing the shells of millions of
minute marine creatures), they had been
reworked by the action of the tides.

Page 106 DRAWING INSPIRATION
A similar theme to that of 'Forgotten Lines'
on page 82, but more of a reflection on
times past and the re-awakening of
memories, as old correspondence is burnt;
watching long forgotten words fade to
black and disappear.

Page 114 REVEALED LINES 2
I've written on page 137 about the transitory
quality of contemporary communication.
These lines evolved from that notion and are
about the stonemason's craft as he teases
words out of the stone with mallet and chisel.

Page 124 DOWNFALL
High Abbotside and Cotterdale are favourite
destinations when I visit Yorkshire. In 2005 I did
a number of paintings based on this area and
the drawing on this page was for one of them.
The poem describes the extraordinary slabs of
rock piled up beneath a waterfall.

ARCH OF STONE EXPOSED
BY THE LONG INCLINE OF TIME.
CHALK AND FLINT, BONE.
MOUND OF EARTH LONG GONE.

TALL GRASS AND COLOUR ROCK
HEAVY, HELD BY THE CLUTCH
OF SKY, AIR, WATER, STONE.
SCORCHED BY SUMMER FIRE.

REVEALED
LINES 1
58x48cms
2006

Revealed Lines

REVEALED LINES 2
40x41cms
2006

Revealed Lines

The two paintings 'Revealed Lines 1' and 'Revealed Lines 2' on pages 134 and 136 respectively were the result of concerns that I felt about the permanence of contemporary electronic communication. Our past, particularly our social and domestic past, is well documented. We can still read the letters originally written on wooden tablets by Roman soldiers stationed at Hadrian's Wall around AD 100 or Paul Nash's letter to his wife from the trenches in March 1917. The soldiers, unsurprisingly unimpressed by our climate, requested that more warm socks be sent to them. In his letter, Paul Nash wished to receive the poems of Edward Thomas, (then published under the name of Edward Eastaway). It is these details, the minutiae of life, that illuminates the human condition. Now that the email, the telephone and texting have virtually replaced letter writing, so much of our actual daily experience will be lost for ever. Responding to that sombre thought I created these two paintings and also the poems on pages 76 and 114. The concept behind the paintings is that possibly in the far distant future a civilisation may learn more about our ancient past because of the permanence of stone-carved narrative (or even pencil on paper), whereas much of our contemporary social and domestic life is no longer accessible or has been deleted. 'Revealed Lines 2' was also exhibited at the Bournemouth University Art Loan Exhibition of 2007/8.

On page 141 I have included an article about my work which originally appeared in the book 'Fifty Wessex Artists'. It includes a paragraph about the technique I developed in response to the surfaces and textures of the chalk and limestone cliffs of Purbeck. The theory had been with me for many years but the practical problems of setting light to paintings in one's house are obvious and it wasn't until I had my own large, isolated studio that I felt able to safely experiment with fire and paint. The action of extreme heat on paint can be

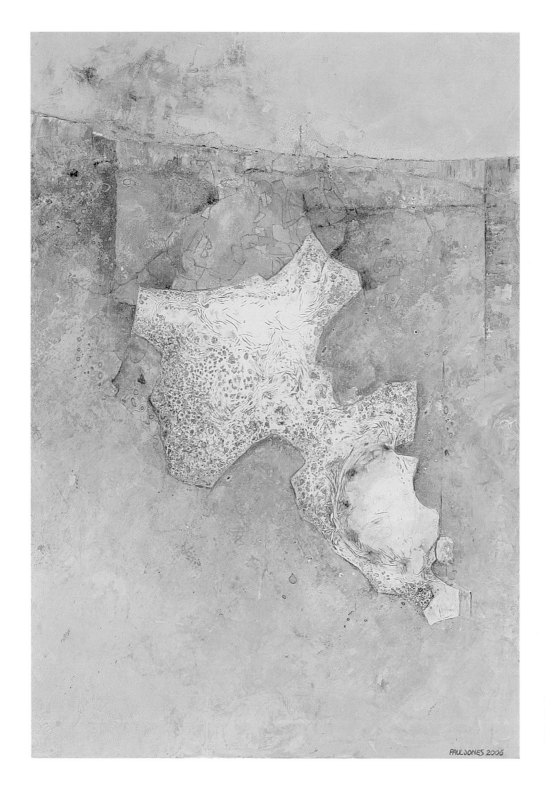

CHALKFIELD
DOWN 2
37x27cms
2006

138

BENEATH
THE SURFACE
92x61cms
2006

ROCKFALL 3
30x20cms
2006

Revealed Lines

extraordinary. Different paints and accelerants all produce different results, for instance a fast, intense burn can transform Prussian Blue into a textured, rusty orange quite unlike any colour that pigment can produce. However, any technique is a means to an end, a process that endeavours to convey truth, and not be an end in itself.

'Techniques will vary, art stays the same, it is a transportation of nature, both forceful and sensitive.'
Claude Monet 1840-1926

The following article is reprinted from the book 'Fifty Wessex Artists', published by Evolver Books in 2006.

'The landscapes of Dorset, the Isle of Purbeck and Cranborne Chase are an infinite resource to which Paul Jones constantly returns. Ancient sites, and locations with evocative names: the Dorset Cursus, Ackling Dyke, St Aldhelm's Head and Winspit, feed his inspiration. On a typical day he will walk many miles with sketchbook and camera, using 'the selection process of the camera lens', backed up with pencil studies and colour references. His sketchbooks are increasingly becoming 'workbooks', used to develop ideas and compositions from his photographs and drawings.

Studio-based, his current paintings are becoming more planned now; the constructed nature of the image-making taking much longer and increasingly informed by the processes of ceramics. Jones lays down base colours and white acrylic on board and then sets it alight. The extreme heat affects the polymer acrylic in a great number of ways. Through experience he is able to control the stresses on the paint and produce surfaces which can be manipulated and moved around before they eventually blister. The textures range from the roughness of sandpaper to bubbles which can burst revealing the colours underneath.

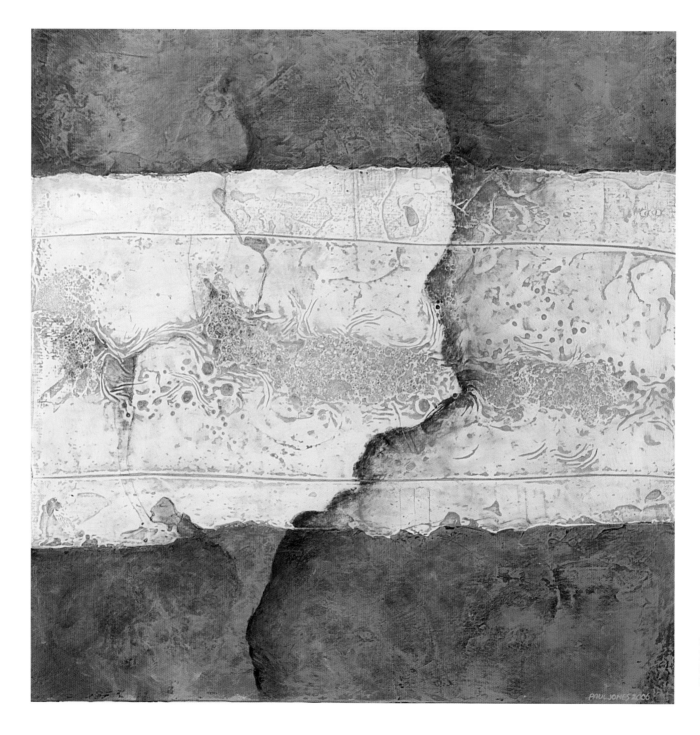

UNCERTAIN
EDGE
26x26cms
2006

142

Revealed
Lines

Once it is completely dry, he can smooth it down, cut into it, and rub in more colour before repeating the process.

His palette is subtle: earth colours, umbers and ochres, soft violets and mauves, blues, olive green, Naples Yellow, rusty oranges and occasional touches of emerald. The tonal range is deliberately limited. White dominates, partly as a reference to the chalk of his chosen landscapes, and partly because of the nature of the paint itself. This unique technique allows him to 'get close to the natural surfaces' which are his inspiration.

Poetry; TS Eliot, Dylan Thomas, Rebecca Elson, and music, in particular, jazz, are his other passions. *Out of the Blue*, one of a series of paintings inspired by Miles Davis, is based on a single trumpet phrase. A strip of liquid blue paint glows above a rectangle of striated colour; the two together form a square which floats on a mesmerising ground of rich darkness like a note hanging in the still air.

More usually it is visual stimuli which informs Jones' compositions. The stacked pale forms and scored marks of *Coastal Observation* suggest slabbed stone which has split and ground against itself, creating complex fault lines. The indentations resemble the pitted textures of chalk cliffs and strips, top and bottom, and have the quality of polished marble. In *Downfall*, curving forms are built up on surfaces of pale silver blue, pockmarked like the carapaces of fossilised creatures. These paintings are 'born out of time and heat', his extraordinary making process replaying the creation through destruction of the ancient landscape which is his subject.

Copyright Fiona Robinson 2006

Article reproduced with the permission of the author and Evolver Books. (See pages 170 and 171).

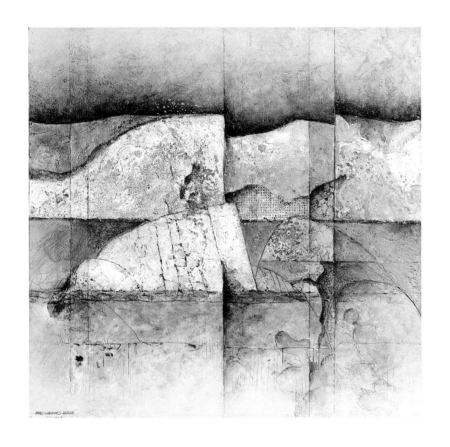

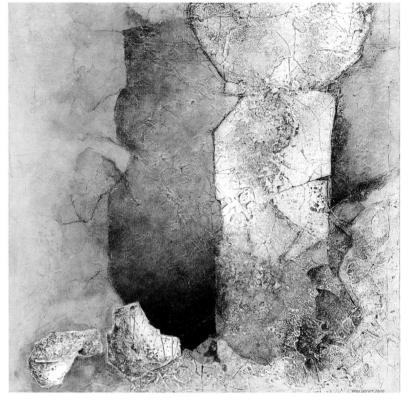

UNSETTLED SURFACE
40x41cms
2006

ROCKPOOL
46x46cms
2006

COASTAL RETURN
36x80cms
2006

Through my wide window
I watch the machines as they rise
vertically and repeatedly, striping
my once and again green hill;
gold and brown, gold and brown.

Framed in my field of vision and
underlining the seagull sky, they
casually create a work of art.

FIELD OF VISION

CHALK DIVISION 2
60x60cms
2006

SEPARATION 2
30x60cms
2007

WHITE EDGE
30x60cms
2007

A chance contact,a
movement in the air,
an unguarded touch.

The minute black berry
swells and spills and
draws a graphic line.

Bright crimson now
but secret, dark, the cross
that marks the thorn.

BLACKTHORN

SILENT
WORKING 2
70x70cms
2007

151

PAUL JONES 2007

CHALKFIELD
60x60cms
2007

152

LANDWORK
53x53cms
2007

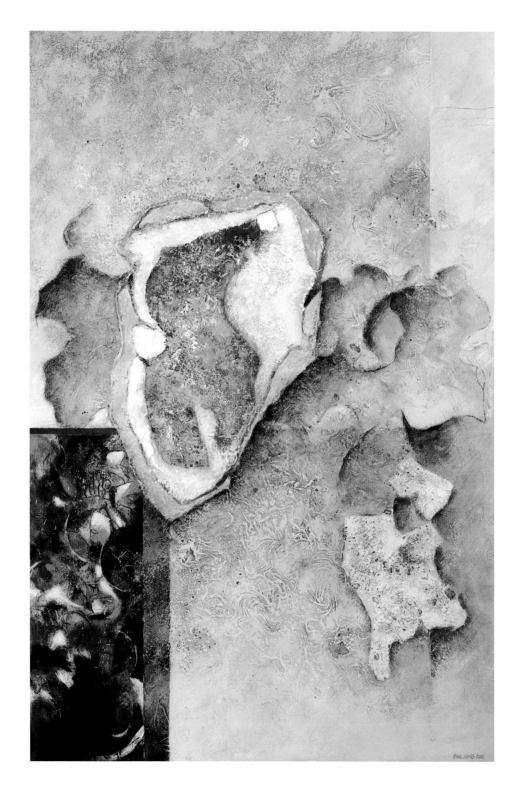

FLINT
75x50cms
2007

EARTHWORKING
80x50cms
2007

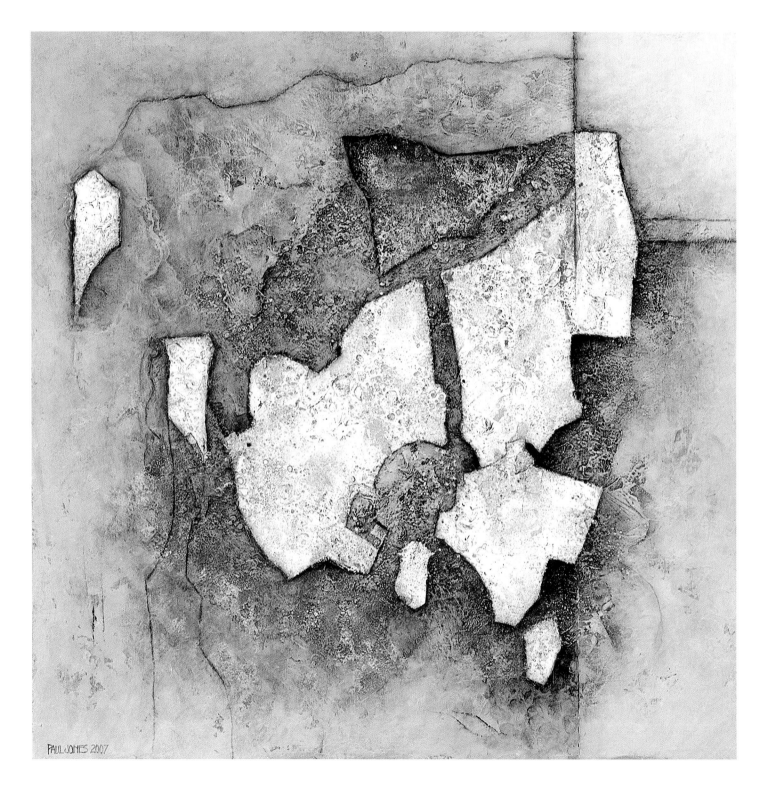

OVERVIEW
60x60cms
2007

156

Revealed Lines

Fiona Robinson's article mentions my interest in jazz, also reading and writing poetry. Music and poetry have a language that is beautiful and complex, full of subtleties, degrees of emphasis, richness of sound and constantly evolving. Personally I associate poetry more with painting because I can participate in the creative process; it is the actual use of language that moves me. What I appreciate about music is its diversity, its ability to suit all moods and the technical virtuosity that is far beyond my capabilities.

The poems I have chosen for this book were the responses to particular experiences, made much in the same way as I would record an image in my workbook. Usually they are an integral part of the creative process with words and images complementing each other. For example, opposite my studio window is a fairly steep hill. One day a red tractor arrived to cut the hay and as it moved up the hill in front of me it appeared to be rising vertically, creating vertical stripes. I drew this and also wrote the few lines on page 146 as it was still working. Other less physical stimuli will produce a response. The poem 'Drawing Inspiration' on page 106 is about memory. While burning old correspondence I was reminded of a similar activity many years before…

TURNING CIRCLE
47x23cms
2007

Revealed Lines

A poem, like a drawing, will be a response to a stimulus that must be recorded and, as with a painting, be worked on, revised and developed in the studio. Initially a poem is a 'drawing in words', an attempt to create an image or emotion in the reader's mind. In looking through my workbook I see notes and key phrases which try to catch the moment and describe a particular experience. Our language is so diverse, a palette of words, colourful, direct, thoughtful, bleak or joyful, changing meaning through association and emphasis. It would be impossible here to list all the poets whose work is on my shelves but I have to name Ted Hughes, Philip Larkin, Edward Thomas, Dylan Thomas, Rebecca Elson and Simon Armitage as most read. My favourite to listen to is Ted Hughes. I've heard that poets in general aren't the best readers of their own work but Hughes' reading of his own poetry, the 'Crow' series for example, is unforgettable, and I much prefer his interpretation of T S Eliot's 'The Waste Land' to any other. It has been said that a successful poem should say in a few lines what a page of prose would convey; as with a painting it's often what is left out that makes that which remains so effective.

During the period 2007 to 2010 I exhibited for the first time at Innocent Fine Art in Bristol and for the last time at Bettles Gallery which finally closed in 2008. The work shown at Innocent expressed my involvement with landscape and coastline. Over the years my paintings had become less place specific and more about the 'landscape within', also the actual painting as an entity in itself became much more important. The visual vocabulary gathered through the years formed the basis of what had evolved into abstracted landscapes. For example, the only references to Cranborne Chase in the paintings on pages 151 to 153 are the exploration of the graphic element in the tracks and field patterns taken from drawings and photographs.

CHALKSTACK 4
75x50cms
2007

ROCKFALL
76x100cms
2007

TURNING POINT
46x60cms
2007

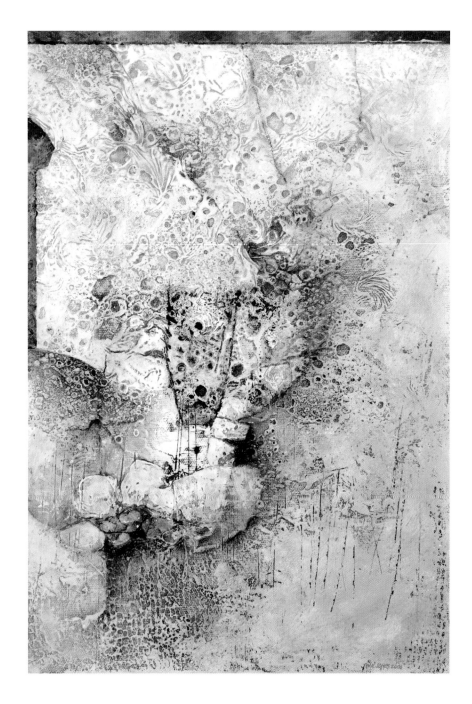

STONEWORK
37x25cms
2008

HEADLAND 2
46x46cms
2008

Revealed Lines

I also isolated and intensified prominent colours and enclosed them in shapes, again selected from my references. Apart from 'Lateral Movement' on page 92 this series came closest to how I could express my involvement with the area. The other piece that became a personal favourite was 'Turning Circle' on page 158, a direct overview of field shapes with a swirl of turning tractor track, my graphic response to a utilitarian action... The 'coastal' paintings, for example, on page 145, (which refers to the balance between sea and land as I mentioned on page 101) and on pages 147 and 149, were also about creating localised areas of graphic detail and contrasting them with broad areas of structured colour and texture.

In 2008 I exhibited for the first time at The Biscuit Factory in Newcastle. Reputed to be one of the largest commercial galleries in Europe it holds exhibitions by invited artists from all over the United Kingdom. I have thoroughly enjoyed visiting Newcastle and have made many friends there. One day I hope to explore the cliffs and headlands of the Northumberland coast which they tell me have an affinity with my work. That first exhibition was very successful and I have been invited to show at the gallery twice since then.

In 2010 I exhibited at the Sladers Yard Gallery in West Bay, Bridport with Brian Graham and John Hubbard. It was good to be back in Dorset again.

FLINTWORK
80x80cms
2008

QUAY OBSERVATION 2
25x38cms
2008

Quicksilver sliding
Waves overtumbling.
Lunatic nightshow
In the bright light
White circle of the
Moon-spinning sky.

MOONDANCING

WHY I
COME HERE
60x60cms
2008

EXHIBITIONS 2007-2008

2007
Bettles Gallery, Ringwood, Hampshire.
With Stephen Murfitt, Ceramics.

Innocent Fine Art, Clifton, Bristol.
With Chris Hankey, Painter.

Bournemouth University.
Art Loans Exhibition.

Bettles Gallery, Ringwood, Hampshire.
Group exhibition.

2008
Acanthus Gallery, Wareham, Dorset.
Group exhibition.

Bettles Gallery, Ringwood, Hampshire.
Group exhibition.

The Biscuit Factory,
Newcastle upon Tyne.
One man exhibition.

Alpha House Gallery, Sherborne, Dorset.
Group exhibition.

BIBLIOGRAPHY

LETTERS OF THE GREAT ARTISTS
Edited by Richard Friedenthal.
Thames & Hudson, London.

PAUL NASH. David Boyd Haycock.
Tate Publishing, London.

PUBLICATIONS

ART LOAN CATALOGUE
Bournemouth University.

FIFTY WESSEX ARTISTS
Evolver Books, Sherborne, Dorset.

EVOLVER MAGAZINE
'Portfolio' feature.

POETRY

FIELD OF VISION Page 146
From my studio in Devon I watched a red
tractor cutting hay on the steep hill opposite.
At one time it appeared to be rising vertically,
then moved on, making intricate linear
patterns in alternate colours. I had watched
a masterpiece in progress…

BLACKTHORN Page 150
Walking on Cranborne Chase one day I
inadvertently spiked my arm on a Blackthorn
bush. The blood grew into a small black berry
before breaking and sliding down my arm in
a graphic red line. Blackthorn can cause
quite serious infection, but not that time.

MOONDANCING Page 168
On November 2008 we went to the Leonard
Cohen Concert in Bournemouth. Afterwards,
walking up to the top of West Cliff we looked
down to the sea and saw the reflection of
the moon, caught up in the incoming tide.
It was a magical sight, a full white moon in a
huge black sky and the moon again, dancing
in the waves.

FIFTY WESSEX ARTISTS features the work of professional artists
currently working in the region. The book includes interviews, images
and studio portraits and was published in 2006 by 'Evolver', the
magazine that supports and promotes the Arts in Wessex. Simon
Barber, whose inspiration is behind both magazine and book says,
'We wanted to build on the success of the magazine by publishing
a book that could celebrate the quality and originality of the
region's most exciting artists'.

FIONA ROBINSON, the author of the article on
page 141 is an artist and writer based in Dorset.
She exhibits internationally and in 2007 won the
University of Bath Painting Prize. In the same
year she was awarded third prize at the
International Drawing Biennale in Melbourne,
Australia. She was Writer in Residence at 'Evolver'
magazine and author of 'Fifty Wessex Artists'.

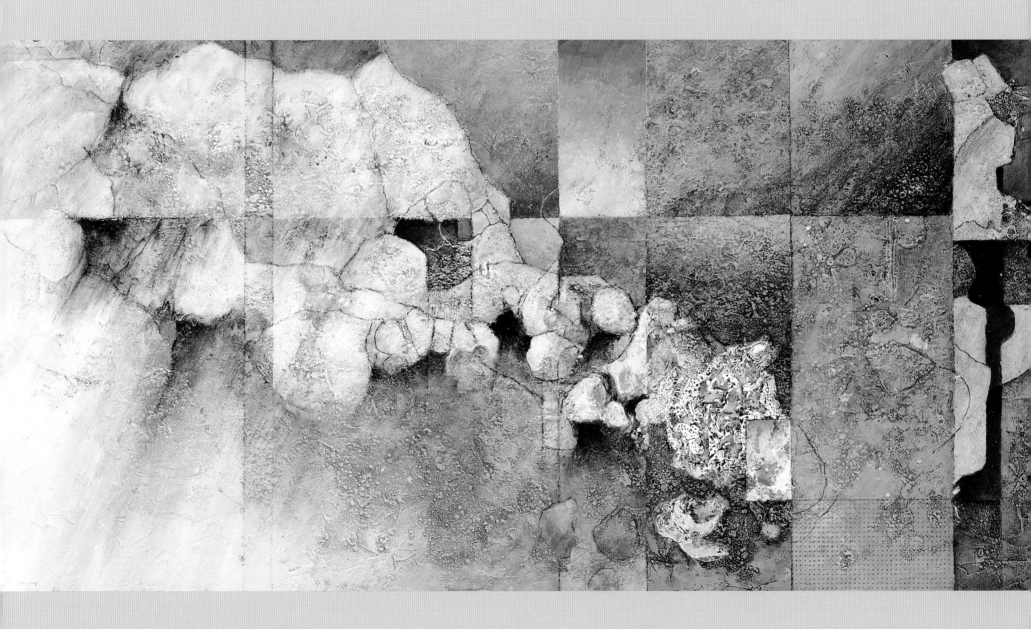

COASTAL DIVISION 2
50x102cms
2008

So Lightly Here

CHALKSTACK 2
76x51cms
2008

So Lightly Here

Why 'So Lightly Here'? Those of you who know Leonard Cohen's work will recognise the phrase from 'Boogie Street', featured in his album 'Ten New Songs'. It is because we are 'so lightly here' that this book, and no doubt countless others, has been produced.

I have been creating paintings for most of my adult life. The collection in this book is selected from the hundreds that have found new homes and some which stay here with me. There are a number of pieces over the years that have a special place in my memory. It is a real sense of achievement when a work is appreciated so much that someone wants it to become a part of their life. It can also be a real ache when paintings go away for ever. What is it that makes a painting work? In my opinion it is when the concept becomes a reality, the imagined comes together, and an image is created that is more than anticipated. Sometimes it can happen as if it is meant to be. 'Fracture' on page 112 is a good example. The flights over Yorkshire had made me aware of the differing shapes of stone walled sheepfolds and their location in the landscape. A whole series of paintings evolved from this concept, the shapes of the constructions being manipulated and abstracted, linked with the landscape as on page 115 and culminating in the simple abstract 'solution' that was 'Fracture'. I have it here in my collection and I wouldn't part with it…

Other paintings became important because they were innovative at the time, to me at least. For example, an experimental use of colour or technique that succeeds, possibly with totally unexpected results – the 'happy accident'. My practice is to recognise it as such and leave well alone.

My selections from recent work are 'Why I Come Here' on page 169, 'Time to Go' on page197 and also

Layered in light, dragged
out and down. Stone release,
fractured, sharp as flint.
the soft clay yet unworked.

Down again sliding, and again
the clutch and pull of time.
Steel on stone split and void
the hollowed hand unfilled.

CLIFF FALL

STONE EDGE
60x60cms
2008

BREAKAWAY
46x60cms
2008

LANDFORM
35x102cms
2008

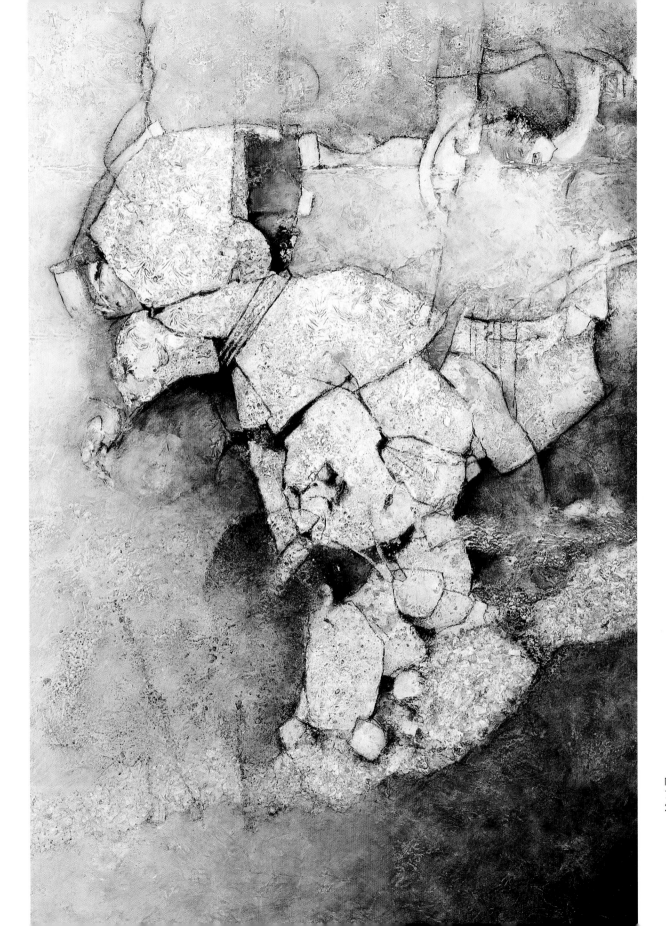

ROCKSTACK
76x51cms
2008

So Lightly Here

'Miles Ahead', (a jazz inspired title) on page 198. In these paintings I have become more selective with texture and stronger in my use of colour, both in contrast and graduation. Each one refers to the chalk cliffs of Dorset but is no longer place specific. As Mark Tobey said, 'My imagination it would seem, has its own geography'. Even so, the Dorset coast has been a constant source of inspiration. Experimenting with scale and the relationships of shape, colour and texture is always a challenge and there is something very special about a coastline, the 'edge' of land, the vertical cliffs, the horizontal sea and the vast sky. There are particular qualities where chalk/limestone cliffs appear to reflect the light and with the rise and fall of the coastline, the sheer elevations suddenly dropping into sea-level inlets and coves. It would be fascinating to make a study of the geology of this country's coastline. Even in the south-west the variations are remarkable. Devon is the only British county to have given its name to a geological system known throughout the world; the Devonian Period of 395-345 million years ago. Devon's south coast also includes part of the 'Jurassic Coast' between Exmouth and Studland in Dorset. The north Devon cliffs, literally only a few minutes from my home, are totally different from those of Purbeck. Here they are more 'raised beaches' with Culm sandstone pebbles and stony clay. Further west the coastline changes dramatically at Hartland Quay where the rocks, sheets of sandstone and shale, have been folded and faulted into fantastic shapes and patterns. From there on, southwards into Cornwall the slate-grey cliffs of the north coast become ever more dramatic.

It has been a fascinating project preparing this book and quite nostalgic at times. Often when I look back at earlier work memories are awakened. For example, I had an exhibition at the West Row Gallery in Wimborne in 1978. It attracted the attention of 'South Today' the Southern Television news programme.

CLEARLY SEE
60x60cms
2008

So Lightly Here

The exhibition was opened by Alexander Thynn, then Lord Weymouth. The television cameras had a splendid time panning from his colourful robes to my multi-coloured paintings. All in all it was a very memorable exhibition. He invited me to take some of my work to Longleat and I had a great day as his guest. He showed me around the house and the rooms he had painted, including the famous one 'decorated in erotic style'. He chose one of my larger paintings and as far as I know it is still there. Whenever I look at 'Stones Circling' on page 39, a painting in the same series, I am reminded of that exhibition and the entertaining day I enjoyed at Longleat. I remained in contact with him for a few years and he was very supportive of my work and progress as a painter.

I enjoy collecting paintings and ceramics created by contemporary artists, many of whom are friends of mine. Over the years I've bought and been given some beautiful pieces and each one has its own story to tell. Looking around my studio and home I see works by Alistair Michie, Harry Cliffe, Brian Graham, Peter Joyce, Francis Hatch, Yvonne Morton, Alan Bourne, Sophie Jones and Tom Baugh; Chris Carter, John Maltby, Alan Wallwork, Elaine Peto, Nigel Eveleigh, Matt Jones and many others, including my latest acquisition, an artist's proof of a print by Sally McLaren.

I have a few of my own photographs in the studio as well. They are mainly pieces that have recorded the image sufficiently well that to try to create paintings from them would be pointless. I don't claim any credit for this as I am only an enthusiastic amateur as far as photography is concerned and regard my camera as a means to an end, a recording of an image that I would like to develop into a painting. It doesn't always work out as planned unfortunately. A couple of years ago I spent the day with my camera in a coastal area

Flint edge, black line,
warm walled sienna, the
blue beneath concealed,
cold like ice under sand.

Circling sacred, a ring
around a stone-dead church.
Empty as a skull, bleak and
black against the light.

Facets of flint, beautiful.
Fractured but permanent
broken, graphic, dangerous,
balanced on the edge of time.

KNOWLTON FLINT

BEYOND
KNOWING
107x46cms
2008

STONE SEQUENCE
60x120cms
2008

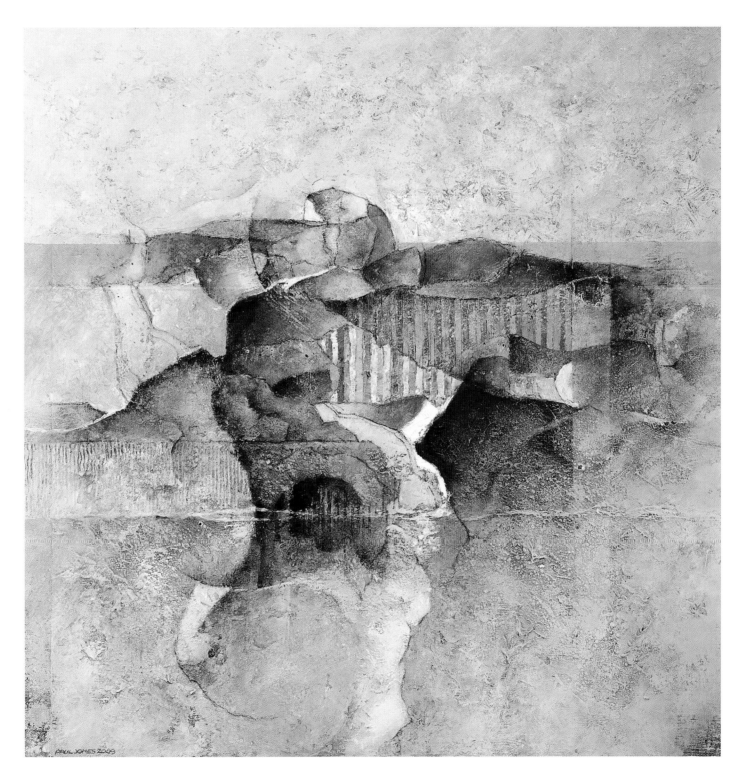

WHERE I STAND
60x60cms
2009

BEYOND THE
SURFACE
46x46cms
2009

So Lightly Here

near Bude in Cornwall called Northcott Mouth. The patterns, colours and complexities I recorded in the rocks were quite extraordinary and I was convinced that the images would be an almost endless resource for a whole series of paintings. Not a bit of it. The paintings were already there in the photographs, already abstract, already nature at its most creative. I destroyed nearly all the attempts I made except for two pieces (pages 16 and 163) and they both found new homes when I exhibited them. One day I'll try again...

In conclusion I will recall the closing paragraphs of my first book. Every painting is still an adventure, and nothing compares to that creative process that drives us on and on, apprehensive of failure but always optimistic of success. No piece of work is ever easy, nor should it be. It is still a mystery that the application of paint and other substances to a surface can create so many meanings, communicate so much and invite so many responses. Paintings have caused riots in France and outraged the 'Red-Top' Press in Britain. Others have inspired great poetry and music, informed us of the life and times of ancient civilisations and religions, been burnt for their unwelcome honesty and worshipped for their symbolism. I am happy that in many homes and places of work many people will today see a painting of mine and hopefully feel pleasure in the experience.

'As I work here in my studio in Devon, with the sun pushing shadows across the hill at me, paint on my jeans and in my genes, I look forward to the work ahead with undiminished anticipation'.

Paul Jones 2010

SEACLIFF
23x56cms
2009

GREEN LANDFORM
36x36cms
2009

191

This stone, cold fragment
lifted from the pale earth,
minute image of the land
around and beneath.

This stone, hard flint.
Soft colours of heat and light,
sharp edge surrounding.
Crafted by time and timeless.

PALE EARTH

GREENCLIFF
60x60cms
2009

193

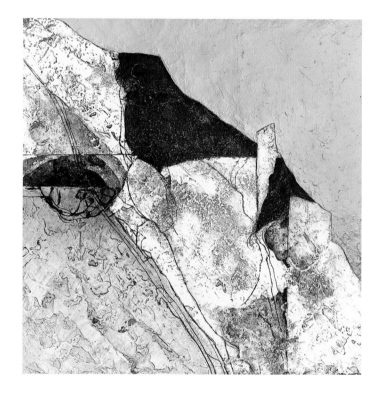

LANDFORM 3
36x36cms
2009

LINEWORK
36x36cms
2009

EXHIBITIONS 2009-2010

2009
The Biscuit Factory,
Newcastle upon Tyne.
One man exhibition.

The Biscuit Factory,
AAF Battersea, London.

2010
Sladers Yard Gallery,
West Bay, Bridport, Dorset.
With John Hubbard and
Brian Graham.

BIBLIOGRAPHY

A WALK THROUGH TIME
Edited by Professor Denys Brunsden.
Coastal Publishing, Wareham, Dorset.

THE PREHISTORIC AGE. Bill Putman.
The Dovecote Press, Wimborne, Dorset.

EXPLORING ANCIENT DORSET
George Osborn.
Dorset Publishing Company, Sherborne.

DEVON'S GEOLOGY. Robert Hoskoth.
Bossiney Books, Launceston, Devon.

PUBLICATIONS

OVERVIEW
Book by Paul Jones

POETRY

CLIFF FALL Page 176
I wrote this poem after watching people
searching for fossils in rocks on the beach at
Charmouth. The cliffs of Dorset are subject
to erosion and in certain areas such land-
slides release a rich variety of fossils, the most
common being ammonites and belemnites.

KNOWLTON FLINT Page 184
Knowlton Rings, situated between Wimborne
and Cranborne in Dorset were originally a
religious centre of considerable importance.
The central circle is occupied by a ruined
church. Flint, being readily available, was in
common use as a building material and this
poem is about a beautiful flint built into the
wall. (See also page 200).

PALE EARTH Page 192
Another extraordinary flint picked up from the
pale earth. Hand-sized and broken, one side
shining with warm and cool colours, the other
side undulating, textured and marked like the
land from whence it came.

HOLD THE
LIGHT
60x60cms
2009

TIME TO GO
76x36cms
2009

MILES AHEAD
50x46cms
2009

PAUL JONES

Paul Jones studied at Bath Academy of Art, Corsham and taught in the Midlands before moving to Dorset. There he discovered an ancient landscape that was to become a lifelong inspiration.

His work was informed by the county's ancient sites and man's 'signatures' on the landscape, the quality of the chalk earth reflecting the light and the complexities of Purbeck's amazing edge, its coastline. The intricate detail and sweeping scale as well as its textures and shapes were all absorbed into his 'vocabulary'. In response he has created new techniques to try and express what he has seen.

He had taught ceramics and that awareness of surfaces and processes, coupled with the need to recreate textures led him to experiment. The experience of firing pots in kilns led him to explore the action of fire on acrylic and oil paint. He learnt about the stresses and textures resulting from this action and by layering, smoothing back and combining with mixed media, managed to achieve the surfaces evident in his paintings, their complex textures contrasting with areas of porcelain-like smoothness.

'These paintings are born out of time and heat, his extraordinary making process replaying the creation through destruction of the ancient landscape which is his subject'. (Fifty Wessex Artists, Evolver Books 2006).

www.pauljonesartist.co.uk

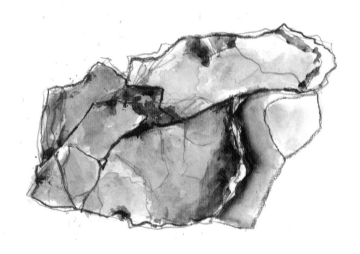

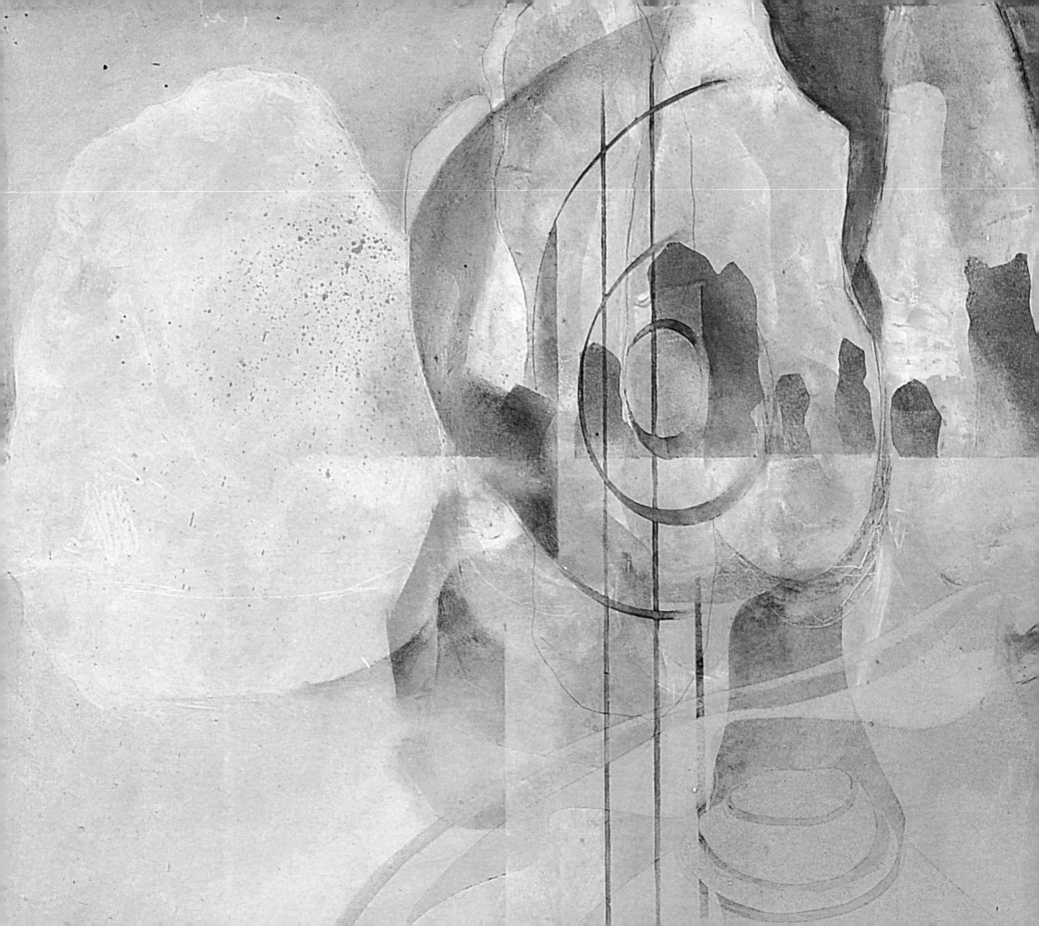